g
Stakeholder Management
into Practice

Springer
Berlin
Heidelberg
New York
Hong Kong
London
Milan
Paris
Tokyo

Margit Huber
Joachim Scharioth
Martina Pallas
Editors

Putting
Stakeholder Management
into Practice

With 64 Figures

 Springer

Dr. Margit Huber
Dr. Joachim Scharioth
Martina Pallas
TNS Infratest
Landsberger Straße 338
80687 München
Germany
margit.huber@nfoeurope.com
joachim.scharioth@nfoeurope.com
martina.pallas@nfoeurope.com

ISBN 3-540-20691-4 Springer-Verlag Berlin Heidelberg New York

Cataloging-in-Publication Data applied for
A catalog record for this book is available from the Library of Congress.
Bibliographic information published by Die Deutsche Bibliothek
Die Deutsche Bibliothek lists this publication in the Deutsche Nationalbibliografie; detailed bibliographic data is available in the Internet at <http://dnb.ddb.de>.

Springer-Verlag is a part of Springer Science+Business Media

springeronline.com

© Springer-Verlag Berlin · Heidelberg 2004
Printed in Germany

Hardcover-Design: Erich Kirchner, Heidelberg

SPIN 10976258   43/3130/DK-5 4 3 2 1 0 – Printed on acid-free paper

Preface

Stakeholder Management in turbulent times

Stakeholder Management has proved to be a useful management tool, even in economically difficult times, as a means for controlling the profitability of businesses and for exerting influence over the different interest groups, such as customers, shareholders and suppliers. The primary concern here is not so much with improvements in customer retention or relations with other stakeholder groups as the economic situation of the business. For instance, measures taken within the framework of customer retention must be directed towards achieving savings without reducing existing customer retention. An intelligent approach to Stakeholder Management is therefore not solely suited to revealing improvement potential, but also conversely to identifying the savings potential that causes the least possible damage to customer relations.

Excepted from this general development are relationships with staff. Businesses that conduct staff surveys as a type of alibi have stopped doing them, whilst others have stepped them up, being aware of the close interrelation between employee commitment and profitability. In these companies, measures to enhance staff commitment are implemented in highly targeted ways.

In this regard, as part of our general research plans, we have investigated the relationship between employee commitment and leadership quality on the one hand, and internal service quality on the other hand. A central result from all of this - at least in Germany - was that leadership quality has an approximately 50% influence on employee commitment. A result of this type was to be expected as a general tendency, but what is surprising about it is how strongly good leaders influence the engagement of the staff and how close this interrelationship really is.

These findings point to the increasing significance of Stakeholder Management. However, in turbulent times every business must focus on the essential, or - as Jack Honomichel, the critical American observer of the market research scene calls it - the imperative data that are indispensable for a business. The payment of bonuses to managers on the basis of performance figures relating to customer satisfaction and employee commitment shows that, thanks to their early-warning character, these data have almost as high a priority as financial data. Stakeholder Management has thus become an important management information system in many businesses.

In a number of businesses, Stakeholder Management has also found its way into strategic financial management where the links between the key figures of Stakeholder Management, turnover and profitability are given far more credence than they previously were.

A further-reaching analysis of worldwide data on Stakeholder Management shows that the direct influence of customer retention on profitability is surprisingly high, at 10 – 20%. Apart from customer retention, however, factors such as the market position of a business, the presence of competitors, pricing aggressiveness in the market and the business's own price positioning and brand play an important part.

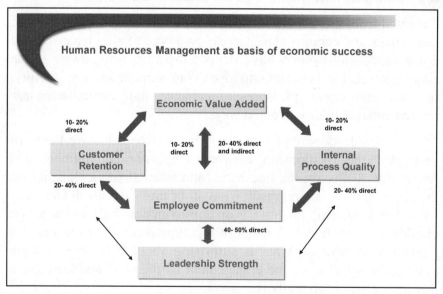

Fig. 1: Human Resources Management as basis of economic success

The design of internal processes is ascribed roughly the same level of significance as customer retention. But, as a result of ever further adaptation of process quality in the course of business reengineering, it has proved to be the case that this has no more influence on profitability than customer retention does.

One is on much firmer ground when analysing the influence of employee commitment on profitability. For an industrialised country like Germany, at least, with relatively high levels of pay and a large degree of engagement by all those involved, employee commitment plays an exceptionally important role in profitability. A direct influence is brought to bear through shorter sick times and through the enhanced performance of committed employees over any given period. However, this employee commitment also has a significant effect on customer retention, on the one hand, and on internal process quality, on the other hand. Committed employees are the basis for every customer retention strategy and they enable even imperfectly designed processes to function, whilst demotivated staff are fully capable of scuppering even the best processes. It is therefore apparent that 20 – 40% of the profitability of a business is attributable to the commitment of the employees, and in some cases this influence may even reach 50%.

Further interesting results have come out of an analysis of the link between employee commitment and leadership. If leadership quality is observed from the standpoint of investigations into stakeholder management, it is apparent that what counts is not only individual leaders, their skilful action and their authenticity, but also that the framework conditions of leadership exert a decisive influence on leadership quality. This has led to the development of a system of instruments that is able not only to measure the leadership quality of an individual person and ultimately to optimise it, but also to analyse organisational framework conditions that are able to function as adjusting factors for the leadership quality of a whole hierarchy level.

A stakeholder group that has never been at the focus of attention although it substantially influences the efficiency of an increasingly leaner business is the suppliers or the outsourced divisions of the business in other companies. As has always been the case, businesses change their suppliers on the basis of relatively small price differences without thinking what costs a change of supplier may bring about in their own organisation. A partnership with their own suppliers enables businesses to utilise many unused cost advantages. It is often the case that greater cost advantages may be achieved by optimising relationships with existing suppliers than through tough purchasing negotiations.

All these examples show how strong the interaction is between the individual stakeholder groups and what an influence they bring to bear on the profitability of a business.

TRI*M which stands for Measuring, Managing, Monitoring is one of the leading branded solutions in the area of Stakeholder Management worldwide.

The articles contained in this volume provide an overview of the variety of Stakeholder Management programmes in different companies. The authors come from Austria, Canada, the Czech Republic, Germany, Switzerland, the United Kingdom and the United States and report on their experiences in managing stakeholders within their businesses.

Since such a publication is a highly collaborative venture, we want to thank all the authors for their enormous efforts they put in this publication.

We are especially grateful to Sabine Kuhnt who has organised the whole layout of the manuscripts. Finally it was very helpful to work with Martina Bihn at Springer who supported the idea of this book from the very beginning and gave us a helping hand whenever needed during the whole process.

Munich, December 2003
Margit Huber, Joachim Scharioth

Contents

X

1 Driving Action with TRI*M

Pauline Williams

1.1 Introduction

Nationwide is the UK's fifth largest mortgage lender and ninth largest retail banking, saving and lending organisation by asset size. More significantly, Nationwide is now the largest building society in the world and is committed to staying mutual. Nationwide has pursued and emphasised this as a viable competitive alternative to 'Plc', 'only for profit' culture since February 1996.

In 2002 Nationwide embarked on a new mortgage strategy – offering all customers (regardless of whether existing, new or remortgaging) the same mortgage products, with an identical interest rate, i.e. no 'special deals'/ introductory offers to new customers at the expense of existing ones. This was in-keeping with the mutuality principle of 'a fair deal for all'. However, initially the new mortgage pricing failed to attract a large number of new customers and failed to retain some existing and remortgaging customers. The Nationwide 'offer' lost appeal amongst mortgage intermediaries too and, as a consequence, Nationwide lost market share.

This, and other factors, led to the setting up of a corporate customer retention programme. This not only covered retention of mortgage customers but retention of all customers *and* employee retention.

At the same time, Nationwide embarked on its iCRM (integrated Customer Relationship Management) programme. The aim of this programme is to build strong, long-term relationships with customers, through better understanding their needs, thereby encouraging further purchase of Nationwide products.

Nationwide's new Chief Executive, Philip Williamson, also launched an internal culture-change programme, PRIDE. PRIDE – **P**utting members (customers) first, **R**ising to the challenge, **I**nspiring confidence, **D**elivering best value and **E**xceeding expectations – provides a framework of attitudes and behaviours for employees to work within. This aims to ensure that all customers (both internal and external) are treated in such a way that they will want to stay with Nationwide and do even more business with us.

To support the retention and iCRM programmes, Nationwide commissioned NFO to conduct TRI*M (internally branded as Commitment) research. The research aimed to inform the business on Nationwide's levels of customer loyalty relative to its key competitors, and what the drivers of loyalty were, in priority order, for each of its core product areas.

1.2   Research approach

1.2.1   Customer commitment

Nationwide commissioned a first stage of research with only Nationwide customers (n=2,300) during the summer 2001. Four core product areas were covered – mortgages, current accounts, short term and long term savings. Customers holding more than one core product with one provider were also studied to understand if their needs were different in any way (multi-product holders). All channels (face-to-face, in branch, phone, postal and internet were covered).

A working party was established, comprising individuals from across the whole business. NFO organised the first workshop where the attributes (anticipated drivers of loyalty) for the questionnaire were derived. Over a thousand attributes were originally thought of, and NFO brought their wealth of experience to bear in reducing the list of attributes to 101.

The first stage of research revealed the key drivers of loyalty for each core product. While the questionnaire had been designed to keep the TRI*M attributes as similar as possible across all products, there was necessarily a degree of variation to accommodate all the differing product features. Importantly, the research revealed that the top ten drivers for each core product (and for multi-product holders) were different. Whilst the top driver was completely consistent across each product area, remaining drivers varied in their order of priority across the product areas and indeed some new drivers appeared in the top ten which were product specific.

This meant that the communication of the research findings would need to be tailored to reflect each particular product area. This suited the organisational structure to a degree, and the market research team delivered a large number of tailored presentations across the business. Incorporated within the presentations were workshops to ensure that audiences could utilise the findings within their business areas.

1.2.2 STARS

NFO and the author have worked for a number of years with Strategic Research - another research supplier that has expertise in managing databases and in data modelling. Most importantly, Strategic Research have a product called STARS which involves the matching of client databases with large quantitative research studies at the individualised level. That is, Mrs Jones' Nationwide record on the marketing database is matched with Mrs Jones' Customer Commitment research responses. The STARS product is compliant with the Data Protection Act and Market Research Society guidelines, since Strategic Research at no point reveal to Nationwide any data which could be individually attributed.

By matching customers' Commitment data with their Nationwide records, individuals can be tracked over time to determine their **actual** levels of loyalty and also whether they purchase further products (see fig. 1 below). This can ultimately confirm the predictability of the Commitment model and should therefore help with the formulation and evolvement of the customer retention strategy. The STARS tracking can determine, for example, whether the strategy should be to move customers from being "retained" to "highly retained", or from "possibly vulnerable" to "retained", to achieve the greatest gain.

4

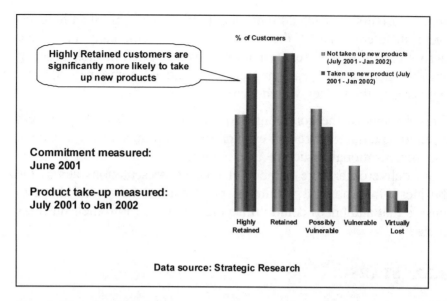

Fig. 1: New product take-up

Over a nine month period, Nationwide ascertained that the Commitment model was indeed predictive and therefore which strategy it should adopt. This information was fed into the iCRM programme and a Brand Relationship Index built onto the marketing database that modelled the Commitment Index onto hard database variables.

By showing the business that the Commitment Index was predictive, it gave the business confidence to invest in a second larger stage of research.

1.2.3 Competitor commitment

Despite the high degree of corporate receptivity to the findings from the first stage of research, it did not reveal how well Nationwide compared with its competitors, thereby rendering any action plans questionable. For example, a key driver for whom Nationwide scores as 'average' might be scored only 'poor' for competitors and thus, in a competitive context, Nationwide efforts to improve an 'average' score might be a focus on the wrong issues.

The Competitor Commitment research was conducted with an existing NFO panel of financial services consumers. This was utilised in order that sufficient numbers of competitor customers could be interviewed at a reasonable cost. Where particular competitor customers for certain products were low in penetration, these samples were boosted. (This meant that the Competitor research could not be matched to the database using STARS, but the first stage had already proved the value of the Index anyway).

The sample structure was similar to that for stage one in terms of products and channels, but now covered the top 3-5 competitors for each core product as well as Nationwide customers. A total of 4,400 'phone interviews were conducted during the winter of 2001/2.

The findings of the research revealed that Nationwide performed better on almost every key driver when compared to its main competitors. The Commitment Indices for Nationwide customers across all the core products were significantly higher than for any competitor.

The market research team communicated the Competitor Commitment Index results across the business to virtually every internal department. Over 680 people were presented to face-to-face, some one on one. Every presentation of the findings was tailored to the particular needs of the audience. Many workshops were held to discuss how to apply the results within individual business areas. The Commitment research was also presented to the Board of Directors by the Market Research team.

This was a great news story and assisted Nationwide in being awarded the Unisys Management Award. It also gave internal encouragement to employees under the PRIDE programme. However, when the results were further analysed against customer *expectations*, all providers needed to improve, even Nationwide!

Once again, it was found that the top ten key drivers did differ in priority depending on which product was being considered (irrespective of competitor). When communicating the results across the business, for maximum impact (particularly at very senior management levels) a strong, clear and consistent message was required across all products. The product driver variants did not allow for this easily.

Consequently, Nationwide embarked on several months of correlation analysis, with NFO calculating how each attribute correlated with every other one. The outcome was a consistent top 5 aggregated drivers across all core products, with a number of attributes being grouped under each driver heading.

This was an important step forward for ensuring that the research findings were embraced by the business as a whole. However, for two of the top aggregated drivers, (referred to later as A and B for reasons of confidentiality) it was clear that the organisation would require further explanation if it was to take action.

1.2.4 Qualitative video research

The Board of Directors requested that the recommendations of the research be presented back to them. To do this, a very impactful presentation was required showing the clear action which Nationwide would need to take.

For each of the top two identified drivers (A and B), Nationwide commissioned another research agency to conduct qualitative research, in order to disaggregate the findings further. By using video clips of actual consumers within the presentation, this ensures that the audience can see for themselves what customers really feel.

This qualitative research led to the development of the Commitment Action Framework. This showed that for Nationwide to continue to build a differentiated brand in the financial services market place leading to superior levels of retention and advocacy, it needed to implement a three-phased action plan.

The first phase concerned delivering 'the basics' of customer service to a high standard. It was felt that Nationwide already did this to a very high degree (with existing business plans already addressing any required improvements).

The second phase necessitated high performance on key driver A – the Action Framework showed *exactly* what 7 corporate behaviours and attitudes this would require, using the video clips to illustrate the point. It was recommended that Nationwide focus on this second phase until a high level of performance could be demonstrated.

The third phase involved high performance on key driver B. However, it was recommended that this phase should not be embarked upon until A was delivered. Importantly, the qualitative research revealed that A needed to be delivered to a high standard before B would be considered credible by consumers.

1.2.5 Senior management buy in

The Commitment Action Framework was presented to the Executive Directors in January 2003. The recommendations were fully embraced and the Chief Executive ensured that there was ownership by two Executive Directors – both in terms of the Action Framework delivery and the dovetailing of the recommendations to the PRIDE programme.

A Commitment Working Group has now been set up under the sponsorship of the Retail Operations Director (who also oversees the Retention programme) and all the prioritised actions identified within the Framework have now been assigned owners. Performance will be monitored by a tailored tracking programme and will be reported bi-monthly to the Board.

1.2.6 Future market research activity

The Commitment programme has been a very significant step forward for the market research team at Nationwide. The Commitment programme has helped to put research on the map. It has enabled the research team to interface with most parts of the business, to drive a major corporate programme forward, provide confidence in research and raise its profile.

The Commitment research also revealed other gaps in Nationwide's knowledge of consumers and, consequently, three other major research programmes have been embarked upon in 2003, each with the potential to be hugely impactful to Nationwide and our customer strategy and delivery.

2 Ten Years of Quality Management at the Hamburger Sparkasse

Andreas Capell

2.1 1993 to 2003 – a quality management process takes on a life of its own

When, in 1993, the idea for "Quality Assurance at Hamburger Sparkasse (Haspa)" was conceived and the first concrete activities for improving customer satisfaction put into practice, no one would have thought that in 2003 the Quality Management Process at Haspa, with all its goals, systems and activities would still be an important and vital factor contributing towards the corporate image of the bank in the Hamburg metropolitan region. But the fact that this is so is documented in the company's mission statement.

We want satisfied customers

The customer is the focal point of everything.

The customer should find us to be a competent, reliable and efficient partner. We in turn should present a friendly and courteous face to the customer.

And we are particularly committed to that.
In over 250 branches and customer centres, we practice "human" banking every day, a service from person to person. This closeness to our customers is our trademark.

> **We want yet more quality**
>
> *For our future success, we need first class, reliable quality everywhere in our Haspa.*
>
> *We are constantly at work on Quality Assurance, so that we can be an efficient partner to our customers over the long term.*
>
> *Our Sales and Back-office divisions work hand-in-hand to achieve this.*

Fig. 1: From Haspa – that's us – our corporate mission statement

For years now, QM building blocks such as quality measurements, complaint management and the creative handling of ideas have been part of the continuously developing Quality Management process at Haspa, in which every staff member can and should be actively involved. After all quality is a central goal for today and the future in the bank's target agreement system, which is equally binding on all employees.

In addition to this, the strategic orientation of Haspa is based on a "quality advantage strategy", which makes clear that Haspa does not seek to win customer loyalty through price, but rather through the quality of its services and products.

2.2 Measuring quality

In a first four-year phase, the branches, centres and departments of Haspa have shaped their own quality work highly individually in "Quality Teams". During this phase, the desire of employees and leaders has grown ever stronger to orient the Quality Management process equally for all involved towards uniform measurement criteria. For this reason, since 1997, a principle that has been in use at Haspa is: *Measure it or forget it!*

2.2.1 TRI*M analyses

For six successive years, Haspa has been measuring customer satisfaction at its branches and Customer Centres with TRI*M, whereby **M**easuring - **M**anaging - **M**onitoring are a firm component part of the Quality Management process.

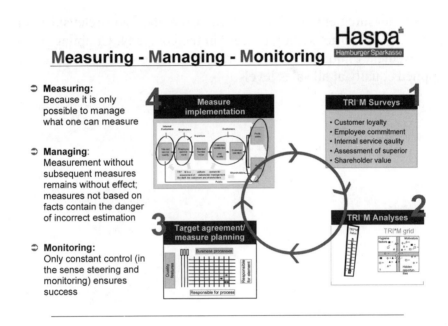

Fig. 2: Measuring – Managing - Monitoring

By means of annual measurements, the branches and Customer Centres can develop their strengths and initiate improvement measures. The aspiration to be permanently oriented towards the needs of the customers is tested every year using a structured testing system: Employing TRI*M as a strategic control instrument.

The results of customer satisfaction analyses are made available to the branches and other centres in the form of clearly readable reports. Starting out as 27 very extensive pages, the reports have now been reduced to 4 pages limited purely to the essential information.

These measurement results are now a remuneration-relevant component of the target setting process in the company. Coupling of the achievement of quality aims to part of a variable salary component is applied equally at all sales levels.

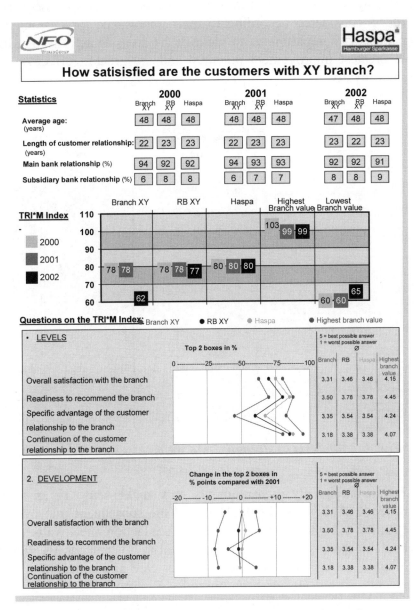

Fig. 3: Representation of the TRI*M index in the branch report (example)

14

An analysis of strengths and weaknesses is oriented towards quality criteria considered according to their importance for customers. It enables sales departments to identify the areas of activity that have the greatest improvement potential and the greatest effect on customer loyalty.

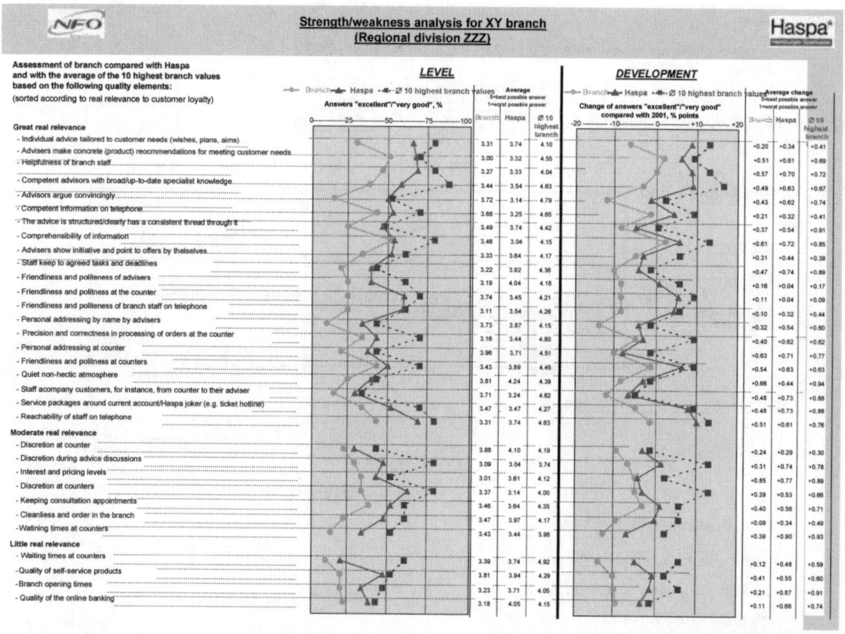

Fig. 4: Analysis of strengths and weaknesses for XY branch

The annual quality measurements only make sense if, as a consequence of their results analysis and the subsequent improvement activities, a higher level of customer satisfaction and loyalty comes about. Haspa has indeed been successful in this respect; through the continual development of our customer care and consultancy competencies, it has always been possible to improve the TRI*M index by a few points over the last few years. Haspa, as the leading retail bank for private, individual and small and medium-sized corporate customers in the metropolitan region of Hamburg has the leading position among its competitors in terms of customer retention. For Haspa, this is the incentive to ensure that closeness to the customers and "human banking" remain a reality for its customers in the future.

2.2.2 Analysis of internal service quality

Haspa quality – count me in! is the guiding motto of the Quality Management process. Since the start of the quality activities in the company, it has been clear that it is not only the external customer who is the focus of the improvement process, so that "only" the employees in sales are "available" to live out customer-focus.

The needs, expectations and quality wishes of the internal customer must also be taken into account to the same extent. After all, a harmonious customer-supplier relationship, particularly between the employees in Sales and the other departments, as well as among the other departments is an important guarantee for successful activity as a customer-oriented sales bank.

Following the successful implementation of the quality measuring instrument in Sales, it has become the focus of Quality Management activities since 2001 to introduce an equally informative quality measuring instrument in the other departments. In this case again, in the first years the employees have been able to take responsibility for – and to work individually on – improvement measures that they themselves regard as being important. When the concrete shaping of the process got underway and the first customer satisfaction analyses followed, the focus of attention was initially on Sales as the direct point of contact to the external customer. Now the other departments are to be brought "up to speed" with regard to customer satisfaction.

The aims of the analysis of internal quality are attuned to the aims of external satisfaction measurements in order to achieve harmonisation between the sales department and the back-office departments:

**Binding design for the Quality Management
process in the divisions**

**Recognition of strengths and weaknesses at the
department level
(= 3rd organisational level)**

Identification of factors relevant to service

**Determination of an index of internal service quality
enables internal benchmarking**

**Monitoring of improvement measures introduced
through follow-up surveys**

Inclusion of measurement results in target agreement process

**Achievement of quality goals is coupled to part of the
variable
remuneration component**

Fig. 5:   Goals of the analysis of internal quality

In 2002, for the first time, internal service quality was measured. A
second measurement, covering 105 departments in 24 divisions and

providing information about possible enhancements of internal customer satisfaction, was conducted in 2003.

Before an internal satisfaction analysis could be begun, the internal customer-supplier relationships had first to be discerned. In a first step, each of the 6000 employees of Haspa was sent a questionnaire online and asked to indicate how often they worked with which department (this acting as a screening process). The scale reached from "very frequently" to "not at all". This relationship matrix, which will have to be updated every year due to organisational changes, formed the foundation of the second step: the main questionnaire itself, also conducted online. Within the framework of this survey, the employees received questionnaire forms for four different departments that were to be assessed.

To ensure the greatest possible degree of anonymity, the satisfaction surveys were carried out in their entirety by NFO Infratest. Haspa had only to supply a list of e-mail adresses and then later take delivery of the evaluations. This also made it possible, during the screening process and the main questionnaire to use reminder mailings, which reminded staff members that they had not filled in their survey forms.

In a similar way to external customer surveys, an index called the Internal Service Index (ISI) is used, which served to indicate the level and structure of internal service quality. The ISI is formed by aggregation of three standard questions:

1. How satisfied are you generally with this department?

2. How would you generally assess the performance of this department?

3. How great is the benefit to your work that is provided by the work of this department?

In addition, the departments receive information on a series of standardised quality criteria relating to their strengths and weaknesses. In similar fashion to an external satisfaction analysis, this strength/weakness assessment forms the basis for identifying areas of action with the greatest potential for improvement and the greatest effect on internal service quality.

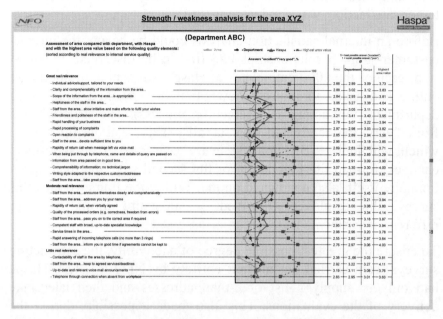

Fig. 6: Strength/weakness analysis for the department XYZ

Internal customer satisfaction analysis has given a strong boost to the Quality Management process in the departments at Haspa. Following initial minor discussions on the content and methods of the survey, staff members very rapidly got to grips with the results for their own division. Strengths and weaknesses were analysed, action requirements identified and measures for reinforcing or improving the results attained were developed. And within a very short time, staff members were engaged in implementing the measures worked out. Everyone was keen to see whether these measures did indeed lead to improvements in service quality.

Particularly during this phase of the first monitoring measurement, it is especially important that staff allow the whole subject of quality to "get under their skin" and affect their personal attitude. Quality must be lived "from the inside out". Assessing the results from a distant position and taking the view that "it's nothing to do with me", coupled with a sense of disappointment about some supposed failure can rapidly lead to a defensive attitude to quality measurement and the whole process. Only those who "program" their attitude to quality and customer focus will understand the measurement results as a small step towards better service quality. Many further steps will follow.

The Quality Management process as a sequence of small steps does not live from passing fads, but from consistent efforts by people to orientate themselves to the needs of customers, regardless of whether they are internal or external customers. Activities undertaken to date in different departments have demonstrated that Haspa is on the right path with regard also to internal service quality.

2.2.3 Mystery shopping

Alongside the satisfaction studies, for several years now mystery shopping has been carried out, and for some time these tests have been mandatory for all branches. In cooperation with an external market research organisation, previously trained testers contact the branches and test both staff behaviour and the specialist competencies of branch employees in a variety of test situations. The test impressions are then stored in a memory protocol and made available to the branches in the form of a report. These test reports form the basis for extensive coaching activities and reflect the actual behaviour of staff and their professional knowledge in the context of direct customer contact. It is therefore all the more pleasing that, over the last few years, the behaviour factors tested at Haspa have improved significantly overall.

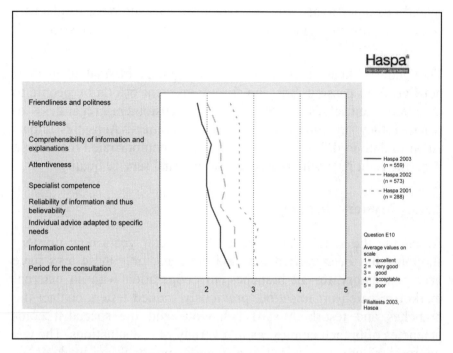

Fig. 7: Assessment of staff behaviour

For quite some time at Haspa, each customer has been advised within the framework of systematic care following a traceable thread that is unique to that individual. With the help of this "guideline", the personal goals of the customer, his personal and financial aims and plans – together with the ensuing results – can be "explored". Building on this information, the advisor can then recommend a financial product corresponding to the needs of the customer.

This consultation philosophy has been accompanied since 2002 by monthly or two-monthly tests with the intention of regularly demonstrating to the branches the success of their advisory activities as well as their improvement potential. The executives use the test results for intensive sales coaching – and with real success; customer care that is both uniformly applied and well structured has been continuously improved over the last two years.

Since mystery shopping as initiated by Haspa reveals only the situation with new customers, for the sake of completeness, surveys of existing customers are also being planned. These more qualitative surveys are intended to provide information about how the conduct of staff and the consultative service they provide are perceived from the viewpoint of "real" customers.

2.3 New customer survey

The new customer survey – carried out since 1996 with small interruptions – was fundamentally reworked at the end of 2002. Using a completely revised questionnaire form, but still applying the philosophy that "your opinion is important to us", the bank is continuing to ask customers who have opened a new current account about their first impressions of Haspa's service quality.

This questionnaire rounds off the extensive spectrum of quality measurements undertaken by Haspa.

2.4 Complaint management

Every customer has his or her own personal expectations of the services provided by Haspa. In the interests of a long-term re-lationship with our bank, it is therefore important firstly to recognise these expectations and then at least to meet them and, best of all, to exceed them. Critical comments from customers make us aware of situations that are unsatisfactory for the customer. We aim to perceive these reactions as an opportunity, rather than an annoyance. The complaining customer is registering a funda-mentally positive attitude to Haspa, since he is taking action to maintain the business relationship. Our task is to grasp the nettle and accept the complaint without reservation. Excellent complaint management often leads to a strengthening of the business relationship.

Aside from the quality standards that are mandatory for all em-ployees with regard to behaviour in complaint situations, principles for successful complaint *processing* have also been worked out.

> **Successful complaint processing takes place
> in the most decentralised manner possible**
>
> **Successful complaint processing is a service task and
> an integral part of leadership responsibility**
>
> **Successful complaint processing requires careful problem
> analysis and thorough researching of the situation**
>
> **Within the framework of his or her possibilities
> every employee must introduce and support measures
> to secure, restore and promote successful cooperation
> with our customers**
>
> **The success of complaint processing also fundamentally
> depends on rapid reaction**

Fig. 8: Principles for successful complaint processing

Building upon our quality standards and principles, the binding nature of the complaint management process at Haspa needs to be documented. However, the written word is certainly not enough on its own to generate a uniform level of understanding among employees with regard to customer-oriented handling of complaints. Workshops for leaders and staff therefore concentrate on the personal attitude of each individual in relation to complaining customers. In these workshops, current complaint situations from daily practice are discussed. Complaint procedures and activities for complaint prevention are covered.

For Haspa, complaint management is an essential building block toward the functioning of a unified Quality Management process.

2.5   The Haspa ideas market (HIM)

The development of the Haspa Ideas Market as an important building block within Quality Management and, whilst serving the function of "internal marketing", demonstrates the pragmatic nature of the development of Quality Management at Haspa.

First considerations in this direction 10 years ago moved towards treating the existing company suggestions system and the beginnings of today's Quality Management as fundamentally two separate processes. Under the situation which then prevailed, the suggestions system tended to motivate individualists to make suggestions with the aim of changing particular processes throughout the organisation.

By contrast, the quality-promoting activities in a large number of Quality Teams in the Sales and other departments pursued collective initiatives. With the help of the Quality Teams, employees were encouraged to consider together how they could become more customer-oriented in their own working domain. In most cases, the solutions worked out in the teams were not generally applicable improvement suggestions that could be used throughout the company, as was the case with the suggestions system, but measures to correct weaknesses in the particular branch, centre or department concerned.

Over the course of the 10-year Quality Management process, the "boundaries" have become ever more fluid. In the HIM of today, an idea is "any concrete initiative and/or any measure successfully tested in one's own area or environment".

Employees have the possibility, using a Lotus Notes database, to "take a stake in" the HIM and to register their ideas. Assessment of the idea, rewarding (or not) of the idea, and implementation of a rewarded idea is all visible to staff members from the Lotus Notes database.

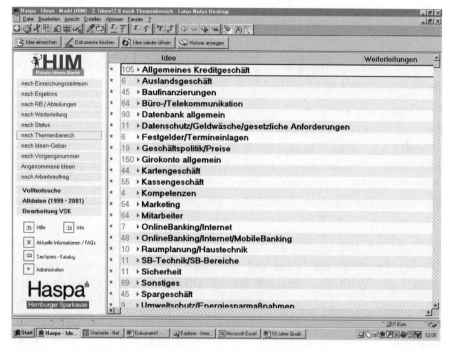

Fig. 9: HIM database/overview by subject area

The Lotus Notes database has become a well-loved internal communications platform. And the fact that entries are not just thrown in without thought is evidenced by the reward payments for ideas that have been implemented. In the first 1½ years since the introduction of the HIM, the payments made for usable ideas that promote the improvements process within the bank have almost doubled, suggesting a new motto: *through creativity to shared success.*

2.6 Summary

The Quality Management process at Haspa has been continuously developed over the last 10 years, drawing in all the employees of the company. Quality measurement instruments, complaint management and the Haspa Ideas Market are key building blocks with which the process is kept up-to-date. Nevertheless, it becomes clear time and again that apart from all the quality instruments, the attitude of every employee towards quality is the most decisive factor in making special service a real experience for the customer. To that extent, even after years of Quality Management activities, again and again staff must be sensitised to the obvious details when dealing with customers: a friendly word, a smile on the telephone – quite simply, giving the customer the feeling that one is there for him or her.

Since the beginning of the activities that comprise the bank's Quality Management system, it has always been clear that continuous nurturing of the Quality Management process, particularly by the management board, gives out positive signals within the company. Through all the improvement measures, notwithstanding how constructively and/or critically they were discussed on a factual level, there has always been a clear signal coming from the management board that says "Yes, we want this!". And that this has contributed significantly to the fact that even after 10 years, the Quality Management process at Haspa stays up-to-the-minute.

3 Driving the Bottom Line in Finance – Is There a Link Between Customer Retention and Business Success in the Financial Services Market?

Elke Himmelsbach, Robert A. Wieland

Abstract

High customer retention is of outstanding importance to all financial institutions. However, during challenging times, investment in the management and monitoring of customer retention is frequently called into question. The rationale for this questioning is that the costs of such activities are often not directly coupled to earnings within a business. But this can be changed.

By developing a company's alignment more towards "customer value management" it is possible to establish a direct link between customer retention and the financial success of the business.

The present article begins by setting out the most important trends in this direction within the financial sector and shows how these are changing the demands being placed on market research.

Its main emphasis is on re-evaluating current hypotheses concerning the links between customer retention and customer value, and profit. Numerous examples are presented from validation studies covering the private and corporate markets in a wide range of financial subsectors, such as banking, insurance and credit cards.

3.1 Development trends

Financial services providers find themselves in a greater state of change today than ever before, due both to changes in customers' expectations and to an increasing dynamism in the market and from the providers themselves. This is an industry that, only a few years ago, felt little incentive to seek more efficiency, but now is becoming ever more aware of the necessity to employ its own shareholder value management. In its attitude to marketing and relationship management, therefore, it is coming increasingly to resemble those industries that have long since found themselves in difficult competitive environments.

Customer satisfaction research first emerged in the financial markets at the beginning of the 1990s, 20 years after the pioneering work of American consumer product research. But this change marked the start of a broad transformation from what had been a supplier's market to a situation where the buyers of financial services are beginning to call the tune. This time delay reflects, in particular, the special market conditions of the industry:

- Customers' decisions concerning many financial products are not taken daily or weekly, but in some cases only once in a lifetime.

- A high level of resistance to change often prevents or lessens any negative effects on business success when customers are dissatisfied.

- Interest and involvement in financial services exists in only a small part of the population compared with other industries. For service providers to private customers, it is therefore often more difficult to create emotional bonds with customers or to change their traditional habits.

By the mid-1990s, the effects of increasing computerisation and internet use on financial service providers were becoming distinctly apparent. The expectations of customers with regard to information and sales routes changed; market entry barriers to new competitors (including online providers such as direct banks, discount brokers and direct insurers) were reduced; the fluctuation of dissatisfied customers was encouraged, at least for a certain proportion of the population. All this has doubtless contributed strongly to the growing importance of customer retention and of loyalty surveys.

The introduction of the EURO was a further influencing factor which prompted many service providers to develop international-ising strategies and inspired them to conduct research into customer needs in the home market. After all, they want to be sure that foreign companies will not find a lucrative niche in their own markets. These fears may be premature, since the customer base of foreign providers remains at a low level in Germany. Nevertheless, cross-border cooperations and mergers of service providers and resultant innovations and changes to customer relations in Germany are bound to become more apparent and more relevant in the next few years. An ongoing investigation by NFO Infratest shows that one in three Germans welcome the fact that foreign financial institutions are entering the German market bringing new services. Foreign companies also serve in many areas as pioneers and as examples in dealing with the problems that preoccupy the financial services industry today.

But what characterises the success of these foreign companies? What factors influence the future strategic orientation of the financial markets?

Today financial service providers need, in particular, to face up to the following trends:

- *Glocalisation*: Alongside the continuing worldwide integration of markets, a concentration on local or regional conditions is also taking place, implying that the key to business success lies in a mixture of synergy effects through harmonisation of worldwide strategy and corporate identity, as well as flexible adaptation to regional needs, particularly in day-to-day business.

- *Future focus with The Balanced Scorecard*: In order to assess the "state of health" of a company, figures from the financial controllership relating to past performance are usually drawn upon. With the Balanced Scorecard, which is being used by ever more financial services providers as a management instrument, monitoring of customer retention as an indicator of future increases in customer value are gaining a growing significance.

- *True customer focus with individualisation - "Mass Customisation"*: In place of product orientation from the provider's standpoint, there is an increasing focus on individual need segmentation from the customer's standpoint. Customer retention comes about through individual customer experiences and therefore calls for a "Customer Events or Experiences Management".

- *Lasting Profitability*: CRM at any price was yesterday's principle. In future, the emphasis will be on holding onto the customer in the face of stronger competition, while simultaneously making the business relationship enduringly more profitable.

For financial market research, this means that today's concern of "customer retention" will become further developed into "customer value management" and that this concept will be paid greater attention at board level in financial service providers.

3.2 New demands placed on customer retention market research for financial services providers

The familiar observation that "all customers are equal but some are more equal than others" reflects a truth that has become irremovably ingrained into sales practice, and even into sales-oriented market research. With the aid of carefully thought-out customer segmentation, it may be shown what relationships exist between the degree of customer retention and actual customer value.

Ideally, customer value takes account of both monetary and non-monetary variables, of turnover and of profit-related factors, and not only of key figures from the past, but also future expectations, for instance, in the context of potential profits and cross-selling potential still to be developed. The difficulty of generating realistic figures, particularly for future and non-monetary dimensions has the result that comprehensive customer value segmentation is still seldom applied in practical market research. According to theory, the following factors count towards this:

a) Market potential encompasses present and future sales success, consisting of

- Earnings potential - i.e. the monetary contribution of the customer to the success of a business

- Development potential, i.e. estimated development of the customer according to life cycle and individual needs, e.g. through changed usage frequency or share of wallet

- Cross-buying-potential, i.e. greater utilisation of further financial products by same supplier

- Loyalty potential, i.e. further use and resale by same supplier, in part with altered price sensitivity

b) Resource potential makes an indirect contribution to business success through

- Reference potential, i.e. by further recommendation. The customer acts as a salesman and, depending upon his personal credibility and satisfaction level, influences others either positively or negatively.

- Information potential, e.g. by positive and negative feedback, within the framework of complaints management or customer surveys.

- Cooperation potential, e.g. through the readiness, as a customer, also to invest in the business relationships with assets and human capital, which is important particularly in corporate customer business.

- Synergy potential, e.g. through the bundling of all products (insurance, savings accounts, payment transactions, securities) in a group of companies or through economies of scale.

3.3 Examples of real cases

Indeed, investigations from a wide variety of financial subsectors reveal clear connections between the aforementioned parameters and the degree of customer retention. The examples and analyses set out below are based on the analysis system TRI*M for Stakeholder Management from NFO Infratest. The customer retention index used for this is based on four variable dimensions: overall satisfaction, further recommendation, continuation or repeat purchase probability and specific benefit compared with the competition as perceived by the customer.

1st thesis:

high customer retention = high loyalty and low churn ✓

In a repeat survey of the same persons with an approximately 3-year interval, it was found that the attitudes and declared intentions in the first wave provide a significant indication of later behaviour. Private customers with a particularly low customer retention index show, in reality, a withdrawal quota far above the average. It is important to realise, in this connection, that fluctuation in the financial market for private customers is still very low, so that that a withdrawal quota of 12% within this period represents an enormous figure (see diagram).

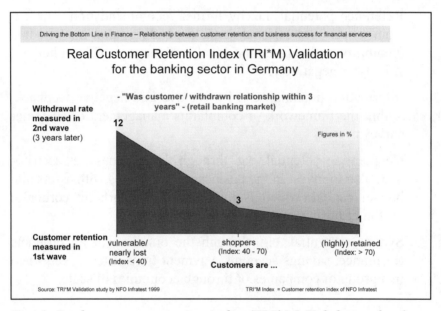

Fig. 1: Real customer retention index (TRI*M) Validation for the banking sector in Germany

Much more frequent, however, are business transfers which, based on a slightly below or above-average customer retention, can flip over into a positive or negative result.

2nd thesis:

high customer retention = high level of cross-buying from the same provider ✓

In practically all customer retention investigations in a wide variety of markets and sectors, it has been possible to verify this thesis. As customer retention varies, so the use of various products and services from the same provider rises or falls accordingly. In the private customer business, this correlation is comparatively weak, due to a high level of exclusive relationships. In the case of online providers, the slope of the correlation curve is somewhat steeper and, in the corporate customer business, as a rule, it is greatest.

At least as important for customer value, however, is the relative turnover or investment volume of the clientele, which leads on to the next thesis.

3rd thesis:
high relative customer retention = high share of wallet ✓

In a worldwide corporate customer retention study for a financial institution, we initially looked in vain for a link to share of wallet (proportion of client turnover to the total business level of the customer). It was when comparing customer retention against that of the main competitor that the difference in customer retention of both providers was first found to correlate to share of wallet (see diagram).

34

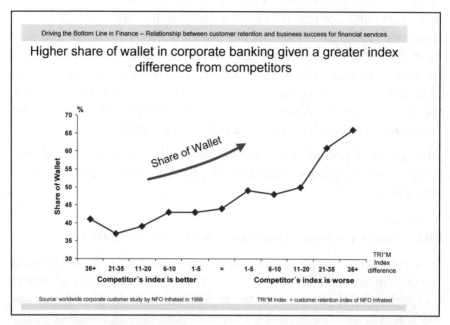

Fig. 2: Higher share of wallet in corporate banking given a greater index difference from competitors

In the end only this makes sense because, when making competitor comparisons, a share of turnover is only ever able to produce complementary results. Customer retention, however, may be equally high or low for several service providers. It is only by gaining the lead over the competition in customer retention that a larger share can be secured and, with it, business success.

Similar results can be found for the private customer business, whether with banks, building societies, insurance companies or credit card providers. Whenever there is an exclusive relationship with a 100% share of wallet, the customer retention index is substantially higher than for financial services customers who have already divided their business between several providers and are thus more easily able to transfer business between different in-stitutions.

There is a further factor that plays an important part in this connection, which is financial potential and the associated expectancy level. When it comes to money matters, "average earners" prefer to make use of one-stop shopping, whilst the "well-off" more often diversify their assets. The same principle applies for businesses, whereby the smaller firms more often have an exclusive relationship, whilst large companies are more likely to have a top-10-list of their most important financial service providers.

But to conclude from this that "high customer retention = low expectations or small financial need" would be a fatal error, since that would be to disregard the extraordinarily high level of competition in the market segment containing financially powerful customers and to lump together very different markets with different requirements.

Share-of-wallet analyses can therefore only be meaningfully interpreted if they focus on a product area and a target group with a relatively homogeneous level of expectations, such as high-net-worth individuals or self-employed people, or the top companies in the Fortune list.

In the field of corporate banking, in place of share of wallet, a ranking analysis of top banks is often undertaken. It can be expected that customers with a first main bank relationship would have a higher retention index than secondary bank customers. And most studies do indeed show this.

However, in the course of investigations we have also discovered a contrary correlation, and this was always the case when the customer base had varying levels of need. Both private and corporate customers usually name, as their first main bank, the institution with which they have daily contact through intensive use of payment transaction services. The requirements placed on such a transaction bank are more easily interchangeable with competitors, while a bank which offers investment services, such as M&A consultancy, is much less likely to have daily contact, but it operates on a higher decision-making level with a greater significance for the customer.

Experience shows that the customer retention index reflects the strategic significance of the customer relationship more strongly than does the frequency of contact. It is only in target groups for whom frequent contact is a real need (and that is the majority of private customers and small to medium-sized businesses for all financial

36

service providers) that there is there a proportional correlation between customer retention and contact frequency.

For some products, contact frequency normally also has something
to do with product utilisation frequency, which also is a distinct
feature of customer value and leads to the following hypothesis:

4th thesis:
high customer retention = high utilisation frequency ✓

The benefit of high utilisation frequency comes from services with
commission charges, e.g. the use of credit cards or online securities
transactions. In normal times - without any special effects - it is always possible to see a significant correlation here (see diagram).

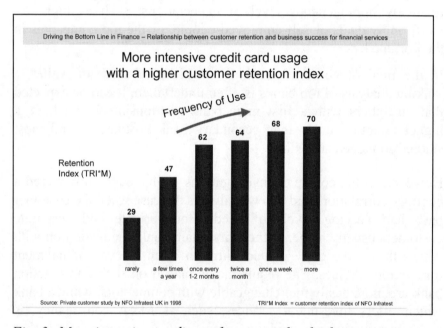

*Fig. 3: More intensive credit card usage with a higher customer
retention index*

Here too, however, it is the exceptions that prove the rule. During
times of sharp stock market falls, for instance, low traders have a
higher customer retention level than heavy traders. The correlation is
generally overlaid by current need changes or recent dissatisfactions,
which have a time-delayed effect on usage behaviour.

5th thesis:

high customer retention = high probability of subsequent business extension ✓

Extension of cooperation with a financial service provider can be observed, measured - as previously stated - from the share of wallet, or independently of the competitive situation. Here, too, the hypothesis can be validated:

Particularly loyal customers extend their business volume with their financial service provider twice as often as other customers (14% vs. 7%). Conversely, only half as many loyal customers reduce their business volume than less satisfied customers (6% vs. 15%).

This is also a result found from a longitudinal analysis for the retail banking sector, whereby the statements by the first group were compared against the behavioural statements made by the second group.

A further variable affecting earnings, apart from turnover volume, is readiness to accept higher prices.

6th thesis:

high customer retention = readiness to pay high prices ✓

It is always said that loyal customers are less price-sensitive. But how can this hypothesis be tested? With the aid of a combination of product-related customer retention analysis and a conjoint method, such as NFO VALUE MANAGER, the connection may be clearly verified.

In the context of an investigation for a payment transaction product, we tested the extent to which there is leeway for price increases. It became clear that the pain threshold for price increases in the case of loyal customers was more than five times as great as that for less satisfied clients.

This strong influence is linked above all to the fact that satisfied and loyal customers do not pay so much attention to price with their financial service providers as more capricious customers do. The reasons for this are generally the positively-perceived "looking-after" and advisory aspects of the respective provider, but often also a lack of price transparency.

By contrast to this, a good price-benefit ratio plays an outstanding part in winning new customers. If one compares old and new customers, it is noticeable that, for new customers, conditions almost always act as a motivator towards customer retention, whilst with the passage of time, they mutate more and more into purely maintenance features.

The aim of most financial service providers - with the exception, perhaps, of the discount brokers, however, is to use price differentiation with existing customers to exploit more fully their earnings potential.

Next, we will look at indirect customer value in the form of the reference and information potential:

7th thesis:
high customer retention = high recommendation rate ✓

Undoubtedly most readers will be familiar with the saying: "A satisfied or unsatisfied customer speaks to x people about his posi-tive or negative experiences and therefore influences new customer acquisition".

This hypothesis was confirmed in our validation study for the bank business. Anyone who is classified as at risk or lost in the customer retention classification has expressed practically no positive recommendations concerning his financial institution. Particularly strongly bound customers, by contrast, advised three actively seeking customers to use their preferred financial service provider (see diagram).

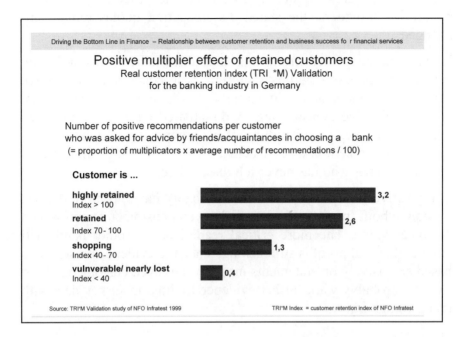

Fig. 4: Positive multiplier effect of retained customers

In this context, it is a relevant observation that good complaints management is worth the cost. Investigations in the banking and insurance industry show that one instance of dissatisfaction can seriously endanger a customer relationship. It is particularly true of a case of dissatisfaction concerning significant customer retention drivers - such as advice that is perceived as faulty - that it results in a lasting worsening of the customer relationship and often leads to a transfer of their business to other service providers.

It is no small customer group that is affected here - in the private customer business of the financial institutions, dissatisfaction quotas of around 20% are normal. And in the very elevated segments that are particularly interesting from the earnings standpoint - but are also very demanding - every second customer feels dissatisfied as often as once a year.

The avoidance of sources of dissatisfaction is one possible route to optimising customer retention. We have discovered, however, that even despite increasing quality assurance and process optimisation by service providers, the stated dissatisfaction quotas remain unchanged.

It may be concluded from this that dissatisfaction is a highly subjective condition and is therefore best countered with active complaints management. Numerous investigations have shown that such an initiative is promising. A dissatisfied customer who is entirely satisfied with the handling of his complaint and with the solving of his problem is usually actually more loyal after this process than a customer who has never felt dissatisfied.

The positively disposed reader will probably have no more doubts, by now, about the individual links between customer retention and customer value. The more critical reader, on the other hand, will counter that real proof is still lacking, since the evidence presented is based exclusively on statements made by surveyed customers. He or she will probably want further evidence by linking survey data with real earnings figures

8th thesis:
correlation between customer retention and real earnings?

Firstly, an analysis requires the bringing together of market research data and statements regarding customer retention and as many further features as possible, along with earnings figures from the database of a financial service provider. The ideal case would be a sound definition and assignment of the earnings for each individual survey respondent.

However, such data are often not available from the clients, and the "second best" solution is then to take the average earnings key figures per branch. This information is always available, as a rule, although it demands the separation of various effects, taking account of the differing customer make-up of each branch.

With the aid of a multiple regression, we firstly established what contribution different factors make to the earnings of different branches. This shows that the profit of individual branches depends primarily on their cost structure and customer numbers (leading to economies of scale) and on other factors that cannot be influenced by the branch, such as the customers' income/assets situation, sociodemographic structure of the customer base, and the competition situation in the locality of the branches.

Once the data had been suitably calibrated for each of the influence factors identified, a relatively strong correlation of r = 0.34 between earnings and customer retention per respondent was found. Finally, it was possible to state that as the variance result, 12% of branch earnings could be explained as resulting from customer retention measured by TRI*M index (see diagram).

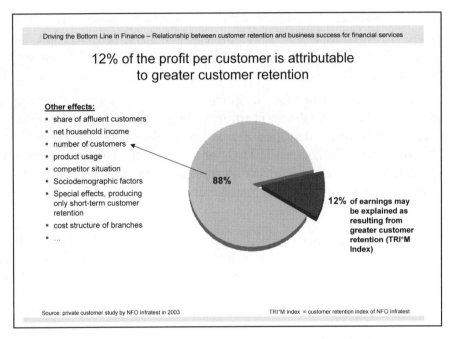

Fig. 5: 12% of the profit per customer is attributable to greater customer retention

Related to the overall profit of a financial institution, therefore, a large earnings potential results from increasing the customer retention, and this in turn provides a justification for customer retention measures in times of tight budgets.

3.4 Conclusions

As service providers, financial institutions operating in an ever tougher competitive environment are dependent upon looking after their customers more thoroughly and thereby using their resources in a more focused fashion. Financial market research gives them individual support by monitoring customer retention intensity for the relevant target segments and by pointing out areas needing attention to enhance customer loyalty.

Since the subject of customer value management looms ever larger in the institutions' action requirements, we have set out what we have learned about the correlation between customer retention and business success.

Based on study results for our client in a wide variety of financial sectors, we have tested a series of hypotheses and "sales arguments" and, in each case, identified a real correlation between the NFO customer retention index (TRI*M) and customer value or business success. It is therefore worthwhile for the industry to continue investing in customer retention management.

4 Customer Retention in Heavy Industry

Martin Platzer

4.1 Brief company outline

voestalpine Schienen, the largest European rail manufacturer with production of over 370,000 tons and a turnover of around € 227 million in the 2002/03 business year is a member of the voestalpine Bahnsysteme group, a division of the stockmarket listed voestalpine AG.

The turnover of the whole voestalpine Bahnsysteme group, which operates a complete value-creation and supply chain across the track manufacturing sector (including its own steel works, rail rolling plants, the points manufacturer VAE operating in 21 locations worldwide, and various project management and service companies) amounted in the 2002/03 business year to about € 1.25 billion.

In the railway track building sector, the companies of the group offer a unique integrated product and service program of the highest quality under the motto "Track Solutions".

4.2 Positioning of voestalpine Schienen

On the one hand, it is true that rails constitute a product with a substantial influence on the safety of the track system (and ultimately of all the rail-bound passenger and freight traffic). Therefore all the manufacturers active in the market must meet fundamental minimum requirements regarding, for instance, the dimensions and material quality of rails.

However, there are substantial technical differences that distinguish voestalpine rails from those of competitors; these include the following:

- Production of the longest unwelded rails in the world (120m) and just-in-time supply according to customer requirements at the construction site
- Some 100 different profiles are on offer, covering the majority of the most important needs throughout the world, including numerous specialities
- Unique patented "in-line" large-scale rail head hardening technology (the HSH® process) in use within the rail rolling process
- High tech quality assurance systems (laser, ultrasound, surface testing using eddy current methods and with fully electronically controlled video systems as a worldwide innovation within the industry).

With these and other performance features, voestalpine Schienen has been able to build up a global reputation as the leader in both technology and quality. An unmistakable market profile has accordingly been developed and publicised, clearly distinguishing the company from other "commodity" providers.

Internally, a consistent policy based on the principles of slim line management structures and the highest possible quality in all departments has been pursued. An important part of the company identity, involving the active participation of the majority of staff, is the Continuous Improvement Process, which has been driven forward in a committed way for a number of years. Several years ago, voestalpine Schienen became the first company in the industry to be awarded ISO certification and, as far as its known, is the only rail rolling works outside Japan to receive JLS approval. The company has been subject to numerous customer system audits and product audits and - not least - has a certified environmental management system.

In recent times, as a part of the voestalpine Bahnsysteme group, voestalpine Schienen has also played an active part in various European organisations and committees with the stated aim of further developing the railway infrastructure through specific projects. The main consideration here is the absolutely essential increase in the efficiency and profitability of the railways - naturally, without any impairment of safety - in the light of the expected increase in rail traffic resulting from the high priority placed on rail travel in EU transport policy (with trans-European networks and corridor projects for better transport connections to the new EU member states, etc.)

4.3   Survey methods and results

Following the selection of the renowned market research institution NFO Infratest, the leader in customer satisfaction surveys with its TRI*M method, as the relevant consultant, joint conceptual development of the survey structure was carried out.

A vital requirement is complete clarity concerning the goals being set and the comprehensibility of the questionnaire form, since this is a prerequisite for the quality and usability of the answers. In order to cover the core European markets, 3 different language versions (German, English and French) were drawn up. Mailing of the questionnaires was undertaken by voestalpine Schienen itself based on an address list from the company's own customer database. The covering letter requested all the addressees to send the completed form back to NFO Infratest, where evaluation was undertaken in a confidential manner. Voestalpine Schienen was then supplied with a conclusive analysis in aggregated form, which did not allow any tracing back to individual questionnaire forms, thus preserving the confidentiality of all the customers' answers.

Some 350 respondents in 14 countries were included and the response rate - in view of the fact that this was the first such survey ever by a rail manufacturer - was more than satisfactory. In the case of customers interviewed by telephone, a full response rate was actually achieved.

The survey included a cross-section of all the important customer groups (railway companies, local transport operators, rail and point manufacturers) with relevant functional subdivisions (e.g. into management, technologists, buyers, etc.).

The results can therefore be regarded as representative in every regard and, happily, they provide voestalpine Schienen with an excellent report, far exceeding all expectations.

Overall, the customers gave voestalpine Schienen a satisfaction index of 90, which represents a seldom achieved top value. In a direct industry comparison, the company also lies significantly ahead of the competition. Over 60% of customers are highly satisfied and loyal (known in the industry jargon as "Apostles"; achieving the largest possible proportion in this group is the aim of marketing), so that voestalpine Schienen also takes the lead by a long margin in the categories of Further Recommendation and Repeat Sales.

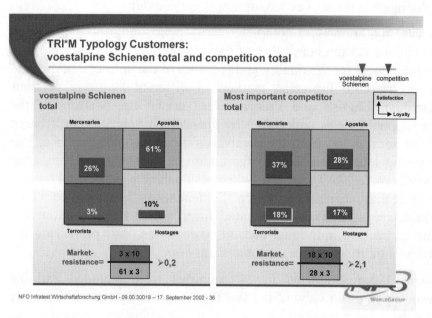

Fig. 1: TRI*M Typology customers

4.4 Operative aspects

Customer orientation and problem-solution orientation are regarded today as principles that no business can dispense with, no matter how remote from its market or bureaucratic it may be.

However, it would be a gross overestimation of the capabilities of customers simply to contract out to an agency the whole presentation of a business to the outside world and to hope that everything will come up smelling of roses.

Not even making the best products is enough on its own to ensure customer loyalty. Rather, a basic condition for success is systematic demonstration of the true capabilities of a business from the viewpoint of the customers.

To illustrate the point with an example, in the case of a hi-fi system, the sound quality is always determined by the weakest components in the audio chain. The best hi-fi amplifier is unable to make its superior performance heard if, for instance, the loudspeakers are not also of a similarly high quality.

It is exactly the same with customer benefit. The sales and customer service organisation must be just as efficient as the manufacturing processes. The same applies to the technology, the logistics, and all other functions of a business. Only when the customer becomes aware of the entire operation as a high quality organisation which consistently acts to serve his interests does optimum customer retention become a possibility.

The feedback control system extends from the requirements that have to be met within the product and service processes through to the customer satisfaction that is their aim and whose measurement, analysis and improvement are also part of the ISO9001:2000 standard. In other words, process-oriented management systems are fundamentally unthinkable without also measuring customer satisfaction.

In the case of voestalpine Schienen, it is self-evident that even highly satisfied customers wish to have greater added value, still more flexibility, more effective and proactive advice, and more intensive dialogue extending beyond the already high standards of the leading customer benefit-provider.

Appropriate measures have now been put in place and are rapidly being further developed.

It should also be mentioned that due to the importance placed on periodic and systematic measurement of customer satisfaction, this process has been defined and documented within the company in the form of an internal procedure agreement.

4.5 Strategic aspects

Industrial marketing has the greatest chance of success when it builds on systematic analyses. There is, as a rule, no lack of statistical data from the past, although its predictive power is very limited. In the dynamically changing markets of today and even more so in the future, early recognition, joint conception and implementation of important developments do now and will in future play decisive roles.

The guiding principle for every successful company must be determined by the aim of creating customer benefit that is superior to that provided by the competition. However, a question that arises directly from this is one of planning reliability. False strategic decisions are difficult to reverse and usually turn into a heavy burden on profitability. Many companies have fallen out of business circulation or become the victims of takeovers by aggressively goal-oriented competitors due to false positioning that has led (often through drastic cost-cutting programs) to unstoppable financial losses.

Constant contact with customers where the information gathered goes beyond pure sales processes is only partly able to cover the necessary decision-making basis. Significant problem areas are:

- is the assessment that has been made really representative?
- is there a danger - due to the usually verbal communication with the customer in these matters - of misinterpretation of a (very

possibly unintentional) subjective bias by the information recipient in the company?

- is there really a consistent picture emerging from the diffuse and fragmented information (because salespeople receive different communications from, say, buyers than, for instance, technologists or managing directors receive from their respective opposite numbers) which will serve as a basis for strategic decision-making?

Only in relatively few cases will it be possible to rely on the information gathered, i.e. that it is truly stable, usable in a reliable manner and future-proof. The consequence is either to make a decision based purely on feeling or, alternatively, for reasons of risk minimisation, not to make a decision, or to make one in too unclear a way, or with too little thought for the future. Both of these options are fundamentally unsatisfactory.

What possibilities remain, therefore, for obtaining the necessary further genuine information for a suitably well-founded strategic decision? A systematic customer survey - provided the right questions are asked - is a helpful measure that is also useful in practice.

Accordingly, voestalpine Schienen worked out a series of strategic questions in cooperation with NFO Infratest, which are grouped together in the section headed "New Services". These include topics that are essential to the future positioning of the company:

R&D strategy: Introduction of a complete new track generation (bainitic head-hardened rails of the DOBAIN® brand) with high resistance to abrasive wear and to rolling contact fatigue damage. In view of the enormous loads that rails are subject to today - and will be to an increasing dègree in future - (including significant frequency increases in rail-bound traffic, higher speeds of up to 300 km/h and further increased axle loading for freight transport), DOBAIN® should represent a technological leap forward and therefore lead to the opening up of further long-term customer benefit potential.

System strategy: What is demanded in this area is customer acceptance of a further intensification of the complete-solution and system-solution range of options beyond product supply (e.g. ultra-long rails in unwelded lengths of up to 120 m, not only supplied just-in-time free at the construction site, but subsequently also unloaded with the company's own innovative pull-off systems) and additional services to round off the existing value-creation chain.

Quality strategy: The question of customers' wishes for further product improvements through, for instance, refinement of rail rolling tolerances and of rail surfaces has been raised.

In all points, the question was asked whether the new service represents a real solution from the viewpoint of the respective client, which he can use and for which he is prepared to make the corresponding payment.

It is clear that such questions are only relevant if a large degree of trust is placed in the survey-conducting company or if the customers recognise voestalpine Schienen as the leading customer benefit-provider. In this case, given the additional cover provided by the individual confidentiality secured by NFO Infratest as a renowned market research institution, a high degree of openness and honesty by the respondents may be assumed. The risk of purely tactically motivated answers, although not entirely ruled out, should be re-latively small.

Conversely, this also means that no customer survey is able to compensate for a faulty or unclearly formulated business strategy. Customers are used to working together with partners who, from their standpoint, are the best and would view any indecision by a supplier in a sensitive area of future-oriented solutions to specific problems as a sign of weakness.

The responses received by voestalpine Schienen in relation to their innovation, systems and quality strategies were extremely positive and represented a valuable confirmation of their current projects.

These include the previously concluded opening of a second fully electronically controlled long rail store in the works in order to be ready for the strongly growing demand for just-in-time delivery of ultralong rails at any time (investment total: € 18 million). A large-scale project already completed by the company's committees is the construction of an entirely new rail rolling mill which uses the latest technology and enables a leap into previously unrealised dimensions of flexibility, precision, etc. (investment total: € 66 million).

4.6 Conclusions

Powerful competencies and resources, forward-looking innovations and a well-founded understanding of customers are among the important factors that contribute to the competitiveness of a business, particularly in hard fought-over and well-developed markets. Business to business transactions increasingly take place on the basis of partnership relationships. Their intensity and thus also their success comes from the ability to deal effectively with individual variety and to fulfil specific customer needs.

Naturally, this also applies to heavy industry, except that in this case for reasons of capital intensity, a particularly high level of sensitivity is required, not only in short-term, but also strategic marketing campaigns.

Integrated marketing with the aim of customer retention must therefore be multi-dimensional, and must be flexibly adapted to changes taking place over the course of time. The following theses relate to this:

Service quality: trust, quality and reliability remain traditional base values, but they must be earned anew daily. Once achieved, these must never become a self-satisfied routine, but rather should be used as a platform for further improvements. The foundation - especially for a market leader so clearly at the summit - should be "the customer has a right to the best service", which should also be suitably clearly communicated.

Quality of relationship: Lasting customer retention in the context of a partnership relationship must be built on a voluntary basis. It is only through endurance based on a convincing CRM strategy that existing and future customer and market potential can be optimally exploited to mutual advantage.

Innovation orientation: Creativity and innovation that benefit customers secure the economic successes of tomorrow. It is of essential significance in relation to the major future-related topics such as life cycle costs or RAMS criteria (reliability, availability, maintainability, safety) to have competent positions today and further to develop these in cooperation with the customer in the future.

System competency: In order to reduce the level of complexity for the customer, the provider must accept more responsibility. In the case of voestalpine Schienen, as with all the other companies in the group, this takes place in that the best customer solutions are sought in an interactive, forward-looking manner and these are then offered following the necessary testing.

This close linkage between future-orientation and reliability in all areas makes voestalpine Schienen GmbH a high performance company from its customers' viewpoint, which - as confirmed in the analysis by NFO Infratest – has been awarded the very highest ratings and has by far the highest proportion of very satisfied and highly loyal customers or "Apostles" in comparison to the industry average.

5 Understanding Customer Retention in Eurotel Prague - TRI*M Index Is only Average...

Lenka Šilerová

5.1 The Czech mobile market

Eurotel Prague is the leading mobile operator in the Czech Republic. In the Czech Republic, which has a population numbering more than 10 million, SIM card penetration is about 85%; user penetration is lower, at about 69% of the population. The majority of customers of all three providers opt for prepaid services. T-Mobile and Oskar are in second and third positions in the market, while Eurotel has consistently remained the market leader, with both the largest market share and the highest revenues.

Eurotel entered the market in 1991 as the only mobile telephone service provider in the Czech Republic, using an NMT network. We remained the sole provider until 1996, when we started to provide GSM network services and our main competitor, Radiomobil, entered the GSM market with the Paegas brand. Radiomobil became a part of the international T-Mobile Group, and in 2002 was rebranded T-Mobile. A third competitor, Český Mobil, entered the market in 2000 with the Oskar brand. Oskar brought low prices and tried to target price sensitive customers. Now, in July 2003, Oskar has a 15% market share and has had especial success in reaching residential and smaller business customers.

The current Czech market is approaching saturation; there are very limited opportunities to sell new SIM cards to genuinely new consumers. The use of more than a single SIM card and the practice of switching between providers have started to become common features of 'mobile culture' in the Czech republic, although churn (customer switching) levels remain relatively low when compared to other European countries. At this time, as we reach the end of a sustained boom in the mobile telephone industry, retention of customers is becoming an extremely important issue. A comprehensive understanding of retention and the determinants thereof represents a significant goal in all research activities pertaining to customers.

5.1.1 A brief outline of the history of TRI*M usage in Eurotel

In Eurotel Prague we have been paying careful attention to monitoring and evaluating our customer retention levels for many years, in a fruitful partnership with NFO AISA. The 'trimization' of the company (to coin a term) has reached a very high level over the course of time. TRI*M Methodology was originally applied to standard customers, meaning end users of Eurotel and competitors' SIM cards; subsequently we extended the use of TRI*M Methodology to include analyses of the decision makers of big corporate customers, and also began to incorporate elements of the methodology in the measurement of point-of-sale performance. In addition, basic TRI*M Questions are now incorporated into nearly all market research projects, better to understand explored areas and to estimate their impact on retention. TRI*M Indices and grids are analyzed in many ways to render increasingly complete pictures of retention motivators for individual segments and customer groups. For this reason, we differentiate TRI*M according to many factors such as levels of monthly expenditure (billing), duration of usage, type of customers, segment, usage of particular services and so on, for the broader purpose of understanding general trends and perceptions as well as evaluating relevance and satisfaction; even employee commitment is expressed via the TRI*M Index.

In earlier years, which were characterized by market development and by efforts to increase the numbers of our customers, we learned of the importance of coverage and quality of the network. This was followed by achieving an understanding of the importance of levels of customer care, prices, and the image of the provider. We observed and evaluated interesting changes in these and other areas, and monitored satisfaction, using TRI*M Grids. Many Motivators became Hygienics through the evolution of the market, while

Hidden Opportunities changed to Motivators. As the leading, pre-mium-price provider we have had many questions and discussions about pricing, about the impact of prices on our TRI*M Index, and about price-to-value perceptions - which have become especially important since the low-cost operator Oskar entered the market. Based on these questions we have modelled many significant relationships, such as the impact of premium pricing on retention. Many analyses have been carried out and many questions success-fully answered. Throughout our long-term history with TRI*M we have also learnt that there are many 'hidden factors' influencing retention which are not measured (or which cannot be measured) using the standard TRI*M Grid. We have become accustomed to regularly evaluating the list of individual items in the TRI*M Grids of individual research projects so as to meet customers' needs as well as internal needs. In conclusion, company understanding and usage of TRI*M Methodology is relatively high.

5.1.2 Newly emerging issues

In these times of market stabilization, a focus on retention and its determinants has become ever-increasingly important. For more than 12 months the development of individual TRI*M-evaluated items has been relatively stable, yet there have been changes in retention levels for individual providers despite only limited changes in relevance and satisfaction with regard to individual items. Such areas as coverage, customer care, and store performance have stabilized and show no significant changes in relevance, having become standard areas where customers presume high performance. In our research we have, of course, continued to keep track of these areas, but our main emphasis has been on image, prices, and some generally problematic issues as repairs, which are inevitably difficult as by definition they are connected with negative experiences. Nonetheless, the TRI*M Grid started to seem less revealing, and we were reduced to guessing what caused the changes in the retention levels of both our company and our competitors. A TRI*M Expert might have argued that there was something missing from the TRI*M Items - but in this case, he would not have been right. NFO AISA invested effort in obtaining lists of factors used by other mobile operators in order to compare them with ours, and found there were no significant omissions.

In fact, we found that the seeming lack of correlation between traditionally important TRI*M Items and levels of churn was simply a reaction to stabilization in the market. Providers now have no significant weaknesses and the competitive fight has become both tougher and more sophisticated. As a result we will have to look for even deeper understanding of both customer retention motivators and explanations for changes. Deeper exploration has been conducted in several areas, where we used lessons learned from qualitative research and from workshops with segment leaders and customer care staff to acquire new items which could better explain the market situation. We were successful in including some items reflecting changing customer perceptions of the market and operators, also covering newly created expectations connected with the entrance of a new international brand - Paegas rebranded to T-Mobile - of mobile operator. This competitor's rebranding had an effect on all customers, changing perceptions of the whole market. We now know that retention is not strongly influenced by coverage, quality of signal, performance of stores, or customer care call centres, nor yet simply by the image of the provider. Perception of the price-to-value ratio is still extremely important, but the perception of 'value' is changing. More sophisticated and detailed issues have entered the retention scene, and we should follow them in research and in the everyday management of our business.

We have started to develop our understanding in more complex areas, too, which could not have been easily solved simply by including a few new items in the TRI*M Grid.

5.1.3 Customer experience

Maybe it sounds self-evident to say that individual customer experience has a higher impact on individual level of retention than more objective areas such as evaluation of prices, coverage, or customer help-line performance. In retention research we started to monitor individual experiences, despite this being rather beyond the framework of the standard TRI*M Analysis. In the course of this we ask customers if, over an appropriate relevant period, they have had any specific, unexpected experiences with their mobile operator (either positive or negative). They are then asked to describe the experience, and to evaluate it in terms of positive/negative polarity. After the first months of this research we discovered some very surprising results: those of our post-paid customers who had had any kind of negative experience showed retention levels which were lower by as much as 32 TRI*M Index points than those who had had a positive experience. This is no small difference.

This research process also revealed differences in the expectations of the customers of individual providers. Customers of the cheaper mobile operator Oskar do not show such significant differences resulting from positive or negative experiences. Negative experiences with their operator (such as billing errors, signal problems, and quality of service) do not have such an impact on general retention levels. They pay less and expect less, whereas Eurotel customers pay more and consequently expect more. Any faults or problems therefore result in a sense of disappointment. Monitoring individual experiences can also help us to see the impact of some of the bigger PR issues, such as the price increases of T-Mobile. It even gives us an idea of newly emergent issues suitable for inclusion in the standard TRI*M.

Learning from several months of tracking experiences in research had led us to the continuing development of a more detailed and sophisticated system of internal collection of customer experiences across different interfaces, and the use of this knowledge in the improvement of our services and processes. The management of customer experience is very important in the conditions of a stabilized, fully developed market.

5.1.4   Marketing communications

The fact that marketing communications, both direct and indirect, influence general attitudes towards the company as expressed in TRI*M is probably also unsurprising, although the influence of this aspect of a company's activities is probably largely unconscious. It is likely that the amount of media exposure, the relevance of advertising messages, the quality of advertisements and other difficult-to-measure variables play a substantial role in customer retention.

We have seen the significant impact of above-the-line communications on the TRI*M Index at Christmas times, which are characterized by extremely high advertising expenditure. A second important demonstration of the huge impact of media communications can be seen in last year's rebranding of the Radiomobil trade name from Paegas to T-Mobile. The massive advertising expenditure connected with building a new brand in the Czech republic led to an unbelievable increase in the provider's TRI*M Index for several months. When, subsequently, media expenditure decreased, the TRI*M Index fell very quickly without any big changes in satisfaction ratings of individual quality elements, except the image characteristics ratings. The failure to meet increased expectations of the new brand (resultant from the massive media drive) probably significantly contributed to the previously mentioned changes in retention levels and increased churn. These examples should motivate us to pay more attention to the relationship between retention, as expressed by the TRI*M Index, and marketing communications (especially above-the-line communications).

To better understand the impact of media communications we integrated a section covering communications (currently only above-the-line communications) into standard TRI*M Questionnaires. Initial results show that some types of campaigns, especially those related to image, have an impact on our customers' general TRI*M Index levels. This impact is a measured (not estimated) difference of about 8 points between those who are aware of a relevant TV campaign and those who are not. However, this is true only for some types of campaigns, and these effects will be further analyzed and correlated with communication results and with the general evaluation of campaign performances conducted through other NFO methodologies.

Currently, we also have other ideas which should be developed for improved understanding of all factors having an impact on retention. Clearly, however, including customer experience and marketing communication seems to have a big potential for creating a more complete picture of customer perceptions, needs and attitudes.

5.1.5 Summary

To sum up, the TRI*M Index expressing retention is an extremely important indicator for mobile services providers in a saturated market. Nonetheless, it is only an average number. More important is to understand what underlies the TRI*M Results, and what controllable and less-controllable factors can have an influence upon it. The TRI*M Grid is one significant part of understanding, but we should continuously think about other factors and should not neglect those individual customer experiences that can hardly be systematically tracked in research. Current conditions demand the use of more and more sophisticated analyses to really understand (and not simply monitor and measure) important motivators of retention. And, of course, understanding is extremely important, but is only the first step. Proper targeting and management of all related activities is also vital.

6   For the Better of the Company: Making TRI*M Work - The Orange Switzerland Experience

Graham Hurst

6.1   The Orange story

Orange is one of the leading global players in the mobile service industry today. The success of the Orange story was far from obvious at the outset. It started its first operation in the UK as the third entrant only. As the mobile service business requires large investments up-front, this is a very significant disadvantage. No (former) fixed network monopoly was available to fund the heavy investment required for the initial build-up of the network infrastructure or the business' international expansion. In summary, structural advantages were hardly available. It seems fair to say that their success can clearly be attributed to the innovativeness of the Orange idea as much as to the ingenuity and dedication of the Orange people, its leaders and its staff.

In Switzerland, Orange was facing a similar challenge whilst launching its mobile services, where it was also the third entrant only. The incumbent player enjoyed a time advantage of approximately six years since its launch. Unlike most other markets with a monopolistic provider, there was no apparent thirst for change. Also, the topology of the Swiss landscape did not lend itself to a quick catch-up in terms of network build-up and coverage.

Orange managed an excellent start, based on a national roaming agreement and a very successful launch campaign. Nevertheless, the reality of being a start-up company caught up with them pretty soon. The TRI*M score of customer retention declined to the low fifties and even lower in specific target markets and geographical areas. Since these difficult early days, a remarkable turn-around has been achieved. Through continuous and persistent improvement, Orange has clearly distanced itself in terms of customer satisfaction and loyalty from the second entrant, which launched shortly before Orange. Also with scores already clearly in the seventies, it has literally wiped out any advantage held by the incumbent operator and most likely will have taken over by the time this book reaches the shelves. In the same way, the churn rate (the share of customers churning to competitors) has declined in line with the improved customer retention intensity measured (see fig. 1). The latter is a clear demonstration of how closely linked the customer relationship management and a company's success in the market can be.

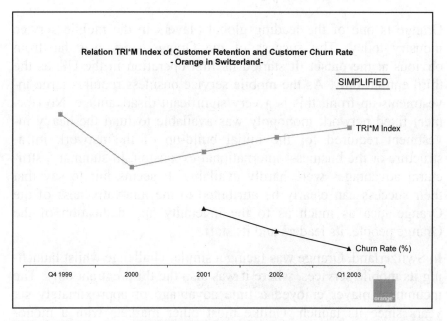

Fig. 1: Evolution of TRI*M Index of Customer Retention Intensity and Churn Rate for Orange in Switzerland - Simplified

Looking back at this point in time, we recognize that the part played by Market Intelligence and more specifically by our TRI*M customer satisfaction and loyalty monitor was probably the easy one. We nevertheless feel that there were many lessons to learn and plenty of experiences to share which might prove helpful in getting on the management agenda and in successfully lending support along the long and stony path to achieving a top performance in customer relationship management.

6.2 Drivers of success

6.2.1 Systems

Max Weber is not the most recent reference in Business Administration. Nevertheless, his point that a modern organization requires some degree of formalization to make it more efficient and more independent from the individuals of the moment remains a fair one. In a similar fashion, a survey or a monitoring tool has all but to gain from integration into a company's system landscape. On the one hand, a company needs to welcome it. On the other hand the tool needs to lend itself to such integration.

6.2.2 Top management priority: TRI*M Index as a corporate key performance indicator

Do you remember the time when Japanese Continuous Improvement Circles became popular in business Europe? A sigh of relief could be heard among ordinary corporate citizens and progressive business thinkers alike. Finally management tapped into the tremendous reservoir of front-line expertise to find solutions to big and small problems, and to spur continuous improvement. What happened to these committees and what happened to this great idea? Don't worry, both are still alive and doing well. They have just developed and matured since then. After some successes of the committees of those early days, many of them appeared to lose their impact on the corporate agenda. Increasingly, attention turned to issues such as "beautifying the reception area with flowers and plants". From there, death and extinction was often not far away.

Clearly, the problem definition is at least as important to success as the problem solving capability itself. In the constant struggle for attention, the need for resources and organizational energy to be in-line with senior management's priorities is essential. As such, the management's decision to make customer retention a key performance indicator not only is a clear commitment to a company's customers, but also defines and communicates effectively its importance inside a company.

In the present case, it was the clear merit of the senior management to decide early on to use the TRI*M Index not only for communicating to shareholders but also as a key performance indicator related to bonuses. This certainly required a lot of courage at the beginning for such a young start-up business, as Orange was at that time. The TRI*M index was, at times, painfully reminiscent of a distant world to be, rather than reflecting real satisfied and retained customers. Also in the world of a start-up business, the hazard and chaos factor gets its own special meaning. Remaining committed to the mid- and long-term vision, whilst balancing this with some short-term frustrations and hardships is all the more remarkable.

Introducing the TRI*M Index as a key performance indicator was a decisive step, focusing attention on customer retention. This attention does, of course, not automatically make every required step a top priority and not every required resource available. But at least it provides a valid reason for requesting resources and a fair chance of being placed on the agenda, even in such delicate areas as IT-resources and systems.

6.2.3 Clear and concise voice: need for a conceptually sound study portfolio

In the mobile telecommunications business, monitoring customers' perceptions of one's own performance and positioning in the market place has become a widely accepted requirement. Just to name a few of the most usual suspects, this includes: Customer Retention, Call Center Performance, Brand Health, and Communication Efficiency.

Studies are conducted on an ongoing basis and are complemented by ad hoc studies investigating specific areas in more detail. In a truly integrated international company, reporting and study requirements come from both levels, local and international. A market intelligence expert will easily distinguish between the nature of all these different studies and the meaning of the different measurements and results. However, this might risk confusing internal clients, who want to work with the results but cannot spend too much time on understanding methodological issues in depth.

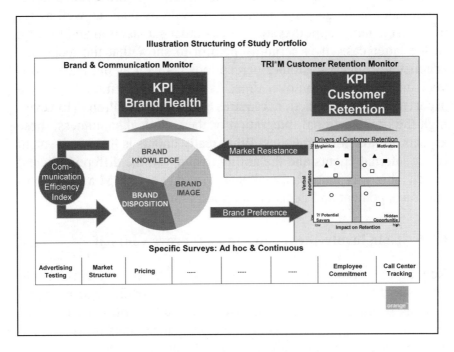

Fig. 2: Illustration structuring of study portfolio

In this context it is all the more important to carefully manage the study portfolio and the positioning and delivery of the results by:

- Properly structuring the study portfolio and consistently communicating the positioning of each survey (see fig. 2 for an illustration)
- Using a limited number of indicators in each area, optimally just one. Avoid the trap of multiplying very similar key measurements because each might give a slightly different

message. Of course each of the key measures should align as much as possible to a Balanced Scorecard approach.

- Closely co-ordinate national and international reporting, by optimally using one single data source, as well as the same reporting periods and measurements.

6.2.4 People

Gaining and retaining credibility and trust within an organization is a constant challenge – for each and every individual, as well as for the management support system of customer satisfaction and loyalty. In the latter case, it is certainly helpful to show that the technique adequately reflects customer perceptions, as well as the market drivers and their evolution over time. Aside from these more techni-cal aspects, human interaction requires the main attention. However, high the organizational integration or the technical soundness, these aspects are just pre-requisites. What really counts is the involvement of the internal clients and the ability to adapt to the different clients' needs. This way there is a real chance to make TRI*M a truly valu-able management and decision support system.

6.2.5 Gain involvement and support: prove yourself

Relying on the common sense that every service company should understand the need for monitoring customer loyalty and act upon insights resulting from it is the wrong attitude. You need to prove the program's capability before the management start to trust it and act upon the insights resulting from it. Doing so is more easily said than done. An opportunity needs to arise first, in order to do so and secondly, the program then needs to live up to the challenge and meet or exceed expectations.

Fortunately, in a start-up situation and in a very dynamic market place, such as the situation presented in Switzerland, there are plenty of opportunities. They often present themselves in the form of emer-gency situations or otherwise unexpected situations in a new market place where experience is only of limited help, for example:

- Management makes a bold decision and enters uncharted waters. All internal indicators show green and the overall situation appears to be stable. Only the customer retention system is able to show that a specific group of customers is about to "jump ship". For example, for the first time, Orange terminates the national roaming-agreement with Swisscom in a specific region, where they consider the build-up of their own network to have made sufficient progress. Only the assessment of the customer perception was able to convince Orange to reverse this move and adopt a more conservative approach for the future.

- An unexpectedly aggressive move by the competition requires urgent and decisive action. Since gambling with one's company's competitive positioning is not an option, the TRI*M system is required to further assess the significance of the situation. This turned out to be helpful, with the help of some additional intensive data analysis and non-standard evaluations. For example, one of the competitors acted very aggressively on prices. The TRI*M study was able to show that Orange had to act quickly but also in a more sophisticated and less aggressive way than just matching the competitor's move.

Whilst the above situations are probably very obvious in a start-up or new market entry situation, they also occur very frequently in more mature businesses and markets. Every new product launch and every new marketing measure is basically a start-up business and a new market entry too, just on a smaller scale.

Other ways of reminding people of the systems' capabilities is to look back and analyze long-term trends and interdependencies. Reflecting what most people already feel in a more objective way and then going beyond the obvious can present an opportunity to create trust. A relatively straightforward case for a new entrant is the long-term impact of network quality or the impact of customer care.

This way, a case history is built up overtime. It might help the company to avoid making the same mistake twice. It also provides a reservoir of anecdotal evidence, frequently more convincing to senior management than a series of abstract numbers.

6.2.6 Involvement: supportiveness and creativity

"It's the people – stupid!" Despite which systems are in place, at the end of the day, it's a company's people that make the difference. People and their experience, qualifications, dedication and commitment, are the single most important factors for the success of a company.

We have emphasized throughout that the system is meant to present a transparent yet sophisticated description of the market situation and its drivers, as perceived by customers. This is necessary to support a creative decision and management process. By no means should it replace the management's strategic vision, the competence and the diligence in finding creative solutions, innovations and in implementing them. We found that a teamwork approach, where every party contributes its following areas of expertise is very helpful:

- the strategy, priorities and most important management decision needs of the company,
- in-depth knowledge of the local market,
- expertise of the industry on a national and international level,
- the market research expertise, and
- Know-how and expertise of the TRI*M methodology.

Only when everything comes together in a relationship of trust and free flowing ideas and information, can the best of designs and reports, interpretations and conclusions be produced. Also, from an overall communication point of view, teaming up and sharing roles can be helpful.

6.2.7 Pragmatism not perfection: each at its own pace

Even in a sophisticated company such as Orange, perfection is not necessarily an every day occurrence. The same holds for the implementation of its customer satisfaction and loyalty program. A certain ability to deal with frustrations or set-backs paired with self-confidence and optimism can be of benefit.

- Quick wins and short-term success are important in achieving business success and maintaining enthusiasm. However, in the end, they alone do not provide the key to success. Not every issue (especially the most important ones) can be solved in a short period of time. Trusting your insights and patient improvement of the main priorities is required. In reward, success may come much faster than expected at the outset.

- Obviously, not every function and not every department is likely to seize the opportunity at the same speed and enthusiasm. The beauty is that there will always be some early adopters, who will use the results and start running action and implementation workshops. This way, success stories are created, which then convince others to follow suit.

The TRI*M program in Orange Switzerland has always benefited from the full support of the senior management. But even in such a favorable case, we found that helping to create and increase the interest within the organization was an important part of the long-term strategy to success.

6.2.8   Self-actualization

Everything is organized. The processes are efficient and smooth, both internally and with the external suppliers. Costs are tightly managed. The TRI*M Customer Retention tracker is happily running along mile after mile, or quarter after quarter. Slowly but surely gigabyte after gigabyte is filled by impressive time series and reports. There is however a good chance that disk space is the only thing that gets populated. What we are really after though is the interest and involvement of our internal clients, and to be put on the management agenda. Continued self-actualization and innovation are the best weapons against a slow but sure death through boredom. Only if (nearly) every new report feels refreshing and exciting, is there a chance to overcome this risk.

The market is in constant fluctuation. So are market priorities. Keeping in constant discussion with internal clients and with external suppliers is essential in constantly keeping study documents and reports focused on these new priorities. While there is a fine line between losing continuity and updating to adapt to changing markets, considering study documents as dynamic documents is essential. The same applies to the involvement of internal decision makers and experts ensuring the relevance of content. Discussions with external suppliers included the updates of questionnaires, but even more so, hot business topics which require further investigation before writing every report.

The company itself is in constant motion - on the international, local, organizational, and individual level. Constant review of the reporting format and delivery method is essential. Every communication of the results needs to be concise and relevant to the audience to keep their interest alive.

The company is progressing along a learning curve. At the beginning "less is more" might be the right motto. This needs to change over time. More and more techniques can be applied or specialized ones developed, for the special purpose of our company. Results can become finer and analyses more varied to help further incremental performance improvement.

6.3 Conclusion

Relying on the TRI*M methodology to support Customer Relationship Management provides an excellent value proposition and a great opportunity. The support of the top management and the integration into the company's key performance systems, are additional important factors for success. But foremost it always remains a people business. The true decisive element to make it a true success story is the gaining of involvement and support, the vision, expertise and creativity, the diligence and perseverance of each and everybody in the company. Keeping this spirit alive and keeping it a success through constant self-actualization and innovation is an exciting journey which never ends. Although this process may become demanding at times, it can also be very rewarding. There is the satisfaction of helping to shape the corporate agenda. But foremost there is the decisive impact of improved customer satisfaction and loyalty on the company's success in the market place.

7 Internal Service Quality as a Critical Factor for Success

Christine Theodorovics

7.1 A general overview of quality management at Credit Suisse

According to the idea of the Service Profit Chain, internal service quality has a direct impact on employee satisfaction and commitment. This, in turn, positively influences customer satisfaction. Employees who work in a satisfying environment, with well-organized processes, effective tools and challenging tasks are inclined to deliver excellent service to customers.

An important finding is that high Internal Service Quality is a prerequisite for employee satisfaction. It is also an essential condition for obtaining customer satisfaction that high quality is delivered in those processes that have a direct impact on the customer[1].

If customers are more satisfied they tend to buy more products or services and this in turn increases the profitability of a company. A successful company is also more attractive for shareholders.

---

[1] Guest speech at the WU-yearly meeting. The detailed results of the researchers were presented on 7.11.2002. (translation by the author). http://science.orf.at/science/news/61486

74

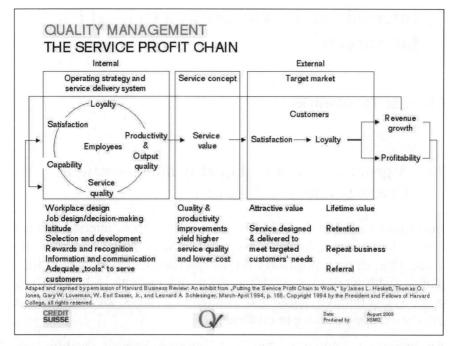

Fig. 1: The service profit chain

Measuring Internal Service Quality is the role of the Quality Management (QM) Department at Credit Suisse[2]. The key tasks for Quality Management are to find out how satisfied clients of the bank are, determine what the service quality is like and identify what could be improved in order to organize processes in a customer-focused way. The Quality Management Department, which forms a unit of the Marketing Department, consists of three organizational subunits: Complaint Management, Service Index and Customer Experience.

The Complaint Management Team is responsible for complaint handling, tracking, reporting and monitoring. The focus is to improve processes and products continuously in order to avoid future complaints. Also the complaint managers carry out a number of edu-

---

[2] Credit Suisse is the second largest Bank in Switzerland and has more than 50'000 employees.

cational modules which help the front staff to handle complaints correctly and which raise the awareness of the client's feedback.

Secondly, the customer view is investigated by the „Customer Experience Team". They analyze very clearly how it feels to be a client of the bank. With different tools such as client observation, simulations and expert assessment of the different interfaces, the team creates interaction maps, which show the present situation as well as the target situation for a specific customer process. The task of Quality Management is to help define the way from the actual to the target experience.

In the third area, Service Index, customer satisfaction surveys are planned, carried out and the results communicated as well as implementation of improvement measures supported. Internal clients are also target persons for such surveys.

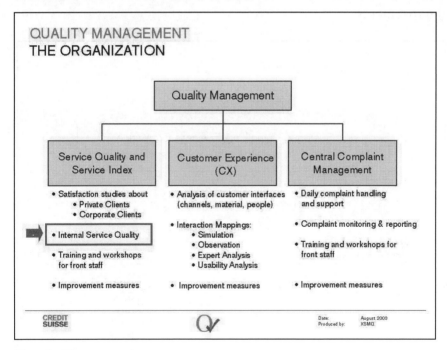

Fig. 2: The organization

For our studies – be it internal or external – NFO Infratest's TRI*M tools have been used for a few years now. For the external surveys, telephone interviews are carried out; for the internal ones the online-method is applied. Many of the results derived from TRI*M surveys form part of the Management by Objective (MbO's) for employees at Credit Suisse. The focus of these surveys is not only the survey results themselves, but much more what happens afterwards with the results. The Quality Management Team regularly supports the different units in defining actions, which derive from the results, and monitors implementation of these actions to a certain extent.

Within the Integrated Quality Management Approach (IQM) the findings of all three teams are combined. In this analysis, all Quality Management data, as well as other internal data, is used to assess the quality of customer processes and to define strengths and areas of improvements.

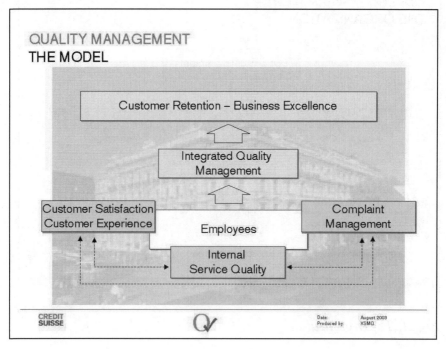

Fig. 3: The model

7.2 Internal Service Quality

With the Stakeholder Management Tool TRI*M, Internal Service Quality is measured with two objectives.

The first is to determine how well different organizational units serve each other. In this method, the organizational units assess each other. The results show where they could potentially and most efficiently improve cooperation, where they already work well with each other, and where departments have a completely different perception of each other.

The second objective is to determine how well internal service centers serve other organizational units. As an example, this could be the assessment of the services provided by a corporate center (i.e. HR, Marketing) by its internal clients.

The first internal quality survey at Credit Suisse took place shortly after Quality Management (a service center) was established and was focused on the Quality Management Department itself. The results of this TRI*M survey were important for the further strategic development of this newly founded unit. Actions for improvement were identified in workshops together with the Quality Management staff. One of the outcomes of these implementation meetings was a series of presentations and communications to raise awareness of Quality Management within the organization. Another consequence was the introduction of a monthly „QM-Tip", which is an aid to the sales-staff and explains „real-life" cases or problems and describes how to avoid such situations or solve them.

Meanwhile a number of internal service TRI*M surveys are carried out at Credit Suisse.

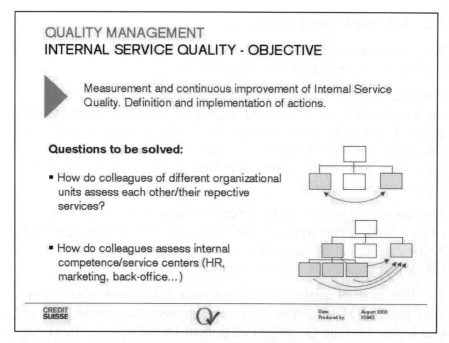

Fig. 4: Internal Service Quality - Objective

Some units need the results because their area of responsibility has changed due to reorganizations or because they were newly established. In this situation, anonymous feedback is of special importance. The results of such a study can be used to identify the acceptance and need of the offered services and products. At such a time, this input is of strategic importance.

Another reason for the rising demand of such data is the fact that a number of departments use a scorecard in order to document their achievement of objectives. Internal Service Quality has more and more contributed to these scorecards.

7.3 How to plan, carry out and use an Internal Service Quality survey

In a workshop where participants of the assessed units take part, the objectives of Quality Management and Internal Service Quality are usually described and put in a context. The next step is usually the definition of 'internal clients'.

We have found out that this phase changes the participants' awareness of service quality and the perception of colleagues as internal customers.

It is, however, not always easy to define all internal touch points precisely. In large organizations it is therefore advisable to use an organization chart when identifying different client segments in the workshops. This ensures that you do not leave out any relevant groups of internal clients.

The quality and usability of the results of the survey depend on the precise identification of the people you want to survey.

Once the identification of the target segments has taken place, the different processes which are relevant in that relationship can be discussed.

The processes, which form the touch points between the internal supplier and internal customer (i.e. sales and back-office), need to be identified and further subdivided into different process-steps. Then, participants in a brainstorming-meeting identify questions which are relevant to assess the level of the internal service quality. Quite a number of the elements included are usually personal issues relating to, for example, friendliness and competence.

At this point, the participants of the workshops often already realize a change in their mindset since the expectations and needs of their internal customers are openly addressed and discussed. The items to be asked need to be selected carefully, since those are the elements that will appear in the strength and weakness analysis. The TRI*M Grid is then the working tool to be used in the identification of actions required and measures to be taken.

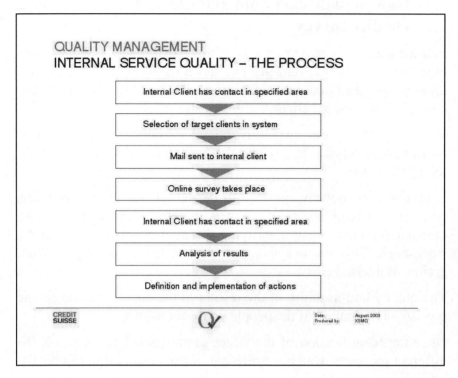

Fig. 5: Internal Service Quality – The process

7.4 Online surveys

For surveys concerning Internal Service Quality, the online-method is almost exclusively used today. Also, at Credit Suisse we chose this method which is easily applied, usable in different languages, which is important in Switzerland, and shows a good price/performance ratio. Once the initial questionnaire has been programmed, only marginal costs arise when changes occur in future surveys.

Our partners at NFO Infratest regularly check our questionnaires and program the surveys. With the help of NFO Infratest absolute anonymity is assured. This is important, since in order to obtain a high participation rate, the survey participants must be convinced of the anonymity. All participants initially receive an email of NFO

Infratest in which the purpose of the survey is explained and absolute anonymity is further assured. Each person receives a personal code with which he or she can access the questionnaire. With the help of this system, it is guaranteed that each person can only participate once, but may interrupt as often as required and continue afterwards.

The person is informed all the time while completing the questionnaire how much of the survey is already completed and how much is still missing. A little column on the upper right hand side shows the amount in percentile of the entire task.

It is important in the entire communication process to stress the fact that the online survey is absolutely anonymous.

7.5 Management buy-in and utilizing results

The most important part of any survey is the management buy-in needed. Needless to say, even a very well organized and executed survey will not be useful if no actions follow. This is only the possible if top management provides buy-in for such a program.

At Credit Suisse, the commitment of a member of top management in the bank helped substantially to apply TRI*M Internal Service Quality within the bank.

Quality Management carried out a very successful pilot study whereby the sales organization assessed the back office.

The results were communicated to the staff as soon as they were available. After the presentation, the decision was taken to include the TRI*M Index in the MbO's of the staff.

Since the pilot survey was a success it was expanded to include the whole of Switzerland and now more than 1000 employees of Credit Suisse have the chance to assess the services and products provided by the back office.

Afterwards, Quality Management actively supported with implementation workshops. In these workshops the results are discussed and actions are defined. This is done on a working level including teams of 3-5 people.

The outcome of these workshops is a list, including the assessment dates and names of the internal service owners and data about delivery of the change.

In defining the strengths and areas of improvement the focus is first on the strengths in the Motivator area (area, where the elements shows high verbal and actual importance). Those items have to be communicated clearly. Then, the weaker points in the Motivator field and the Hidden Opportunities areas with a low verbal importance but a high relevance (impact) on customer satisfaction are examined. Usually not more than 5-8 items are picked out for a workshop. This number provides the base for the definition and implementation of activities following the TRI*M results (see fig. 5).

Surveys of Internal Service Quality are now an established part of the Credit Suisse culture. Nearly 8000 employees will participate in Internal Service Quality surveys in 2003.

Quality Management is responsible for the organization and realization of the analysis. Again the major focus of Quality Management will be on the use of results for quality improving measures within the bank[3].

---

[3] This year a random sample will be used, since more than one survey will take place at the same time. With this method it can be ensured that the same staff member is surveyed three times in a row for three different surveys.

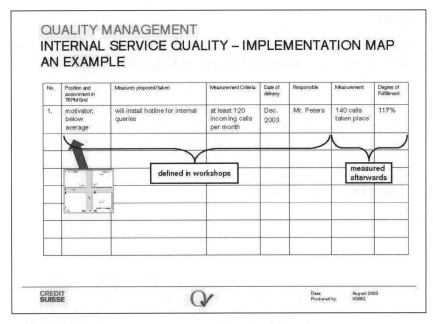

No.	Position and assessment in TRI*M Grid	Measures proposed/taken	Measurement Criteria	Date of delivery	Responsible	Measurement	Degree of Fulfilment
1.	motivator; below average	will install hotline for internal queries	at least 120 incoming calls per month	Dec. 2003	Mr. Peters	140 calls taken place	117%

Fig. 6: Internal Service Quality – Implementation map

7.6 Benefits

Since TRI*M is also used for external customer retention surveys, a comparison of those results with those of the internal surveys is possible. Some of the internal results can well be used to interpret the findings and results better.

Most of the staff concerned with internal or external results is trained to read and correctly interpret a TRI*M Grid, which also helps the spread of information quite substantially.

If one assumes that the employees are the most valuable resource in a company and that employee commitment and Internal Service Quality show a high correlation[4], one can conclude that regular measurements of Internal Service Quality are an important tool to improve the business results of a company.

---

[4] Symposium 17.11.2003, Dr. Joachim Scharioth, NFO Infratest

Literature

- Interbrand Forum (Milligan Annie; Smith Shaun – editors); Uncommon Practice; Pearson Education Limited; UK, 2002

- Sasser W. Earl; Heskett James L., Schlesinger Leonard A., The Ser-vice Profit Chain: How Leading Companies link Profit and Growth to Loyalty, Satisfaction and Value, Free Press, 1997 p. 256

- Smith Shaun, Wheeler Joe; Managing the Customer Experience, FT Prentice Hall, Financial Times, UK, 2002

8 The ATB Journey with TRI*M

Brian Digby

8.1 Canada's financial service sector

In Canada, the financial services sector has been regulated for many decades. As a result, six major banks dominate and years of regulated growth have produced in a stable and highly advanced financial system. According to the Department of Finance, Canada, "Canada has the highest number of ABMs per capita in the world and benefits from the highest penetration levels of electronic channels such as debit cards, Internet and telephone banking."

New legislation in 1999 allowed 20 to 30 foreign banks to compete with the six major banks, a handful of credit unions and a few small financial institutions that were established many years ago. Most of these "little banks" are highly localized and stubborn when it comes to being merged with larger banks. One financial institution that has maintained its independence and unique positioning over the years has been ATB Financial®, formerly known as the Alberta Treasury Branches.

8.2 A short history of ATB Financial®

Established in 1938, ATB Financial® has both longevity and a single-minded focus on serving the needs of the people in the Province of Alberta. A province of just under 3 million people, Alberta began in agriculture but, since the 1950s, has enjoyed a rise in economic wealth from the discovery of substantial oil and gas reserves. Today, it has one of the strongest economies and highest standards of living in Canada, but this wasn't always the case:

- Back in the 1930s in the middle of "Great Depression" in North America, there was a drought in Canada's prairies. Alberta's farmers and ranchers were hit hard - their crops withered and their cattle starved. People in the province were feeling the pinch,

- The big banks located in central Canada (Toronto and Montreal) weren't offering much help - in fact, they were pulling their support so they would not lend money there,

- The Alberta government got involved. They created a new banking system of six branches in 1938 calling them the Treasury Branches - literally, the branches of the Alberta Government Treasury.

8.3 ATB Financial® today

While the Alberta government remains the sole shareholder and owner of ATB Financial®, in 1997 ATB became a Crown corporation run by an independent board of directors and new management. With these changes have come a significant shift in the growth and marketing efforts of the institution. To signal some of these changes, the name was changed in 2002 from Alberta Treasury Branches to ATB Financial®.

Today, ATB Financial® employs over 3,000 staff, has 145 full-service branches and 132 agencies supplying services to 242 Alberta communities. In addition, ATB Financial® has a state-of-the-art call center with 180 highly trained customer representatives and competitive online and electronic banking services.

ATB Financial® commands significant market share of the deposit and investment business as well as the personal loan and mortgage business in the province and is the number one lender for small business and agriculture in Alberta. ATB has managed to secure a position of strength in the Alberta market, despite the dominance of the six major banks in other Canadian provinces.

8.4   How ATB Financial® has become so strong

Back in 1997 when the new management at ATB Financial® was installed, ATB realized that their first goal was to maintain a strong market share by cultivating long-term customer relationships. In 2001, senior management identified three factors that are critical to their success - employee engagement (how happy the ATB employees are with ATB), enhanced shareholder value (which is defined as financial success) and customer satisfaction. At ATB this strategy is called the "Triple Win."

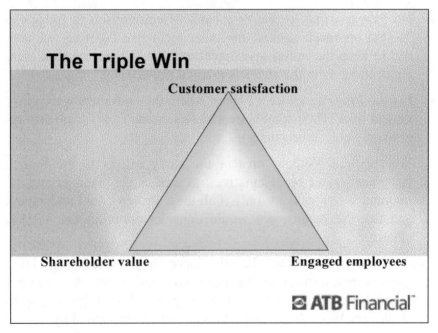

Fig. 1: The triple win

As all key business decisions are made based on this model, it is critical that ATB has ways to measure all three factors. Being a financial institution, measuring financial success is easy and ATB has already implemented a program to measure employee satisfaction. What was needed was a good way to measure how satisfied customers were with the services and products of ATB Financial®.

Up until 2001, ATB Financial® had done little formal customer service research. With no precedents or historical data, we had a blank slate when we approached this initiative. Obviously, TRI*M was the selected approach, but not without some deliberation. NFO CFgroup was a firm we had worked with under their former name (Canadian Facts), so we knew them but not TRI*M. After several presentations, we agreed to test TRI*M in a Pilot study with one of our branches. Some considerations in this step were:

- Hesitation about committing to a proprietary method without first knowing if the approach would suit our requirements for strategic and tactical information,

- No past research to use as a basis of comparison to judge the TRI*M approach against any other methods; therefore, we needed to keep the initial investment in TRI*M low, until we were comfortable with the analysis it could provide,

- For the Pilot, we chose a branch where the customers were fairly typical of ATB customers overall (e.g. some rural, some city types/some old, some young),

- We required NFO to present the study results to the branch customer service representatives, as well as the manager and the regional vice president; only if all these groups could understand and use the results, we would consider adopting the TRI*M system.

Even though we conducted the Pilot survey in just one branch, NFO researchers took us through the entire sequence of steps that a larger study involves. This included the developmental work leading up to the Discovery Workshop - a one-half day session attended by our senior vice presidents, department heads and staff from all areas responsible for client contact. Facilitated by NFO researchers, these 12 people generated a list of over 300 service/quality attributes! Following several iterations to "boil down" the list, we conducted a telephone survey of 300 branch customers using 42 attributes for the measurement.

The branch Pilot went well, so the next step was to do a Baseline study among 27 branches that we felt represented all markets and various branch types. ATB has big branches, little branches, new and old branches located in urban, rural and even remote settings. By completing 300 interviews in each selected branch, we had a large database of just over 8,100 interviews. In the analysis, we gained a full 360 degree of our entire system. Through the TRI*M Index, Typology and Grid analysis, we saw our first "statement" of the health of our relationship with our customers.

As NFO CFgroup conducts regular benchmarking research on the Canadian financial sector, we were happy to see that ATB's Index score competes well with the other major financial institutions in Canada, even though we operate in just one province!

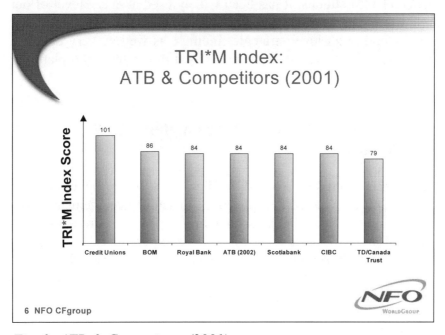

Fig. 2: ATB & Competitors (2001)

8.5 ATB moves to survey all 145 branches using TRI*M

If we were going to be able to use this rich data to guide our improvements in service on a branch-by-branch basis, we knew we needed more data! The "representative" numbers and averages from the Baseline study of 27 branches would not be enough to tell us what we wanted to know. At this point, we could see a need for data specific to each and every branch in order to address service issues at the branch level.

Since the Pilot and the Baseline studies were conducted, we are now in the process of completing our second system-wide TRI*M Monitor study covering all 145 of our branch operations. The first system-wide study was completed in the fall of 2002 and, like the earlier TRI*M studies, it has been widely used at every level of our organization. This has been possible because the TRI*M results provide both high-level strategic findings, as well as very detailed, individual branch results that can be used to create action plans for solving problems.

8.6 Learning from TRI*M throughout ATB Financial®

The results from our TRI*M studies have given us more than insights and knowledge to report back to senior management. From the beginning, when NFO presented the TRI*M Pilot study results to our frontline staff and managers, it was apparent that TRI*M could deliver research findings in a manner easily understood by non-researchers. For example, without any formal training in the background behind the TRI*M Grid analysis, our staff in the pilot branch could identify and comprehend the key messages contained in the results of the research. This was also the first time in ATB history that any marketing research results were presented in person, at the branch level! Since then, we have made extensive use of our Intranet system to share all survey results, including TRI*M, throughout all of ATB Financial®.

To ensure maximum use of our large TRI*M database and findings, we asked NFO to give a number of Microsoft PowerPoint presentations, custom-tailored to various management groups including our Executive Committee of the board, our 6 Regional Vice Presidents and our Product Marketing Group. Each group has used TRI*M to address areas of priority within their span of control. Applications of the TRI*M results include the following:

- For the **Executive Committee**, TRI*M results have spawned a new commitment to customer retention, clarification of our competitive strengths, as well as new business development in fresh markets,

- Our **Regional Vice Presidents** have been equipped with aggregate data reflecting their regional market performance and have used these findings to sit down with the branch managers in their areas, to work out strategic action plans,

- **Individual Branch** "report cards" were prepared and distributed to each branch for review. Following this, discussion workshops were held with branch staff and our manager of research to discuss the implications of the findings for use in tactical planning,

- Finally, our **Product Marketing Group** used TRI*M results to review process weaknesses and identify new product opportunities. They recognize that TRI*M is also measuring what our customers think of our product and service offering, as well as the quality of our service delivery.

8.7 Managing change at ATB

Where is ATB Financial® today? How has TRI*M impacted the way we conduct business with our customers and in our various marketplaces? Simply put, TRI*M has helped us focus clearly on our most valuable relationships, to build on our strengths and to reinforce our unique positioning in the Alberta financial services sector. TRI*M helps point us in the right direction with our precious sales and marketing dollars.

As mentioned, TRI*M fit very well into our "Triple Win" corporate strategy where we take measurement of our progress to secure three elements - engaged employees, a solid bottom line and highly satisfied customers. TRI*M has proven to be a robust measure of our customer satisfaction.

It is also fair to say that the TRI*M approach has also spawned other key components in our customer relationship management strategy. For instance, early after the TRI*M Baseline study, we developed a new customer service model called "WUHAR" which represents a new way of interacting with our clients at all customer touchpoints. Our branch staff and management are being trained in a whole new way of dealing with clients. A simple definition of the WUHAR program is:

- **Welcoming** - our way of greeting our clients by acknowledging them as persons,

- **Understanding** - our goal to fully understand our client's needs and requirements,

- **Helpful** - to be as helpful as possible; simplifying our client's banking and account transactions,

- **Appreciate** - to always thank our customers for their business,

- **Respect** - to always respect our client's privacy, time limitations, and individual circumstances.

The WUHAR principles are the foundation of ATB's personal service positioning. This positioning was recently rolled out as part of a campaign to retain current customers and increase new customers. The campaign selling line "More People. More Branches. More Face-To-Face" captures the core benefit that ATB offers to its customers. We will evaluate the success of this campaign both with custom tracking as well as the TRI*M survey. We will also use TRI*M to adapt the campaign in the future.

In coming years, we may consider increasing the frequency of the measurement from once per year to twice annually or more often. However, for now we recognize that there are several factors that can limit how often we should undertake our TRI*M research. These include the facts:

- That overall attitudes change slowly over time,
- That it takes time to implement system-wide shifts in our service culture,
- The effects of our initiatives may not be evident until customers have progressed through several transaction cycles (e.g. loans, mortgages, investments),
- That customers need to experience multiple banking channels (e.g. branch, Internet, ABM's) to experience the full benefit of our improvement efforts.

In summary, we are pleased with the effects that implementing TRI*M has had throughout our organization. As one of three critical success factors for ATB Financial® (Triple Win), customer satisfaction and loyalty really do drive many of our business decisions. And, we are proud to let the public know that we are listening to them. For example, in our 2002 Annual Report, we state that "By keeping in touch with our customers, we can focus on actions they tell us will enhance satisfaction and loyalty to earn their ultimate compliment ... a referral."

9 A Rather Different Speed Record: From 44 to 90 in Two Years

Horst Schäfers

More, perhaps, than any other industry, the telecommunications business is reliant upon gathering precise information about its customers. After all, hardly any other industry has proved to be as restless and volatile in the last few years as the business of transmitting speech and data. Any operator that is going to hold a steady course in these stormy times must constantly improve its services to keep itself from being pushed out of the market like many other carriers. In 1994 when ISIS was founded, the situation was very different. During that starting phase when the German telecommunications market was just beginning to be liberalised, small, agile, low-priced businesses like ISIS were busy grabbing their first customers from the old unwieldy state-run Deutsche Telekom. In the second phase of market deregulation in 1998, it became possible to acquire private customers as well and there was a real gold-rush spirit among the new companies. However, the cut-throat competition forced prices below any profitability and soon claimed its first victims so that, over the years ISIS, too, had to retreat to its earliest roots and largely leave the mass market to others. As at the start, ISIS is concentrating its efforts on companies, public institutions and administrative bodies once again. The business and the products have also become more individualised and now demand more concentration on the customer. At the same time as this change was occurring, the first regular surveys were ordered from NFO - then called Infratest. The shock was deep when in 2000 a disgraceful TRI*M index of just 44 was recorded for the customer group on which we had particularly concentrated our efforts - the business customers. Now we had in black and white what we had previously suspected: that it was very expensive to change over from the stereotypical private customer mass market to catering for the individual needs of businesses. But to get straight to the point, the latest survey now shows an index for the top segment of our customers of an unbelievable 90. In other words, an enormous amount has changed. How has this come about?

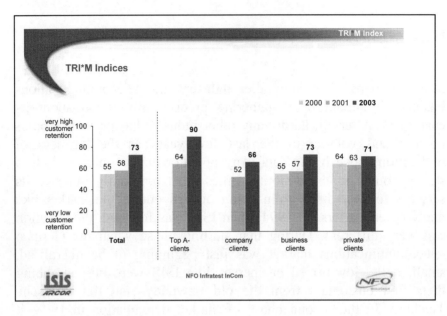

Fig. 1: TRI*M Indices

9.1   A prophet in his own land

"Self-knowledge is the first route to self-improvement", as a well-known German maxim says. It is also the principle by which our leaders attempted to discover and rectify the deficiencies in the company's customer-care mechanisms. As far as the larger business customers were concerned, at first we were missing the target badly. With as many as five contact persons to meet the wishes and needs of this clientele, we were creating a state of confusion. The customer did not want to have to speak to this person about an invoice problem and that person to deal with a connection problem; it proved to be too complicated and impracticable. The curse of what we had thought was our good deed only became clear within the company as the next customer survey brought this muddle to light. Although responsible staff members had previously recognised the problem, they had been like lone voices crying out in the desert. The old saying proved itself once again that a prophet is without honour in his own land, or more correctly as Matthew 13:57b quotes it: "Only in his home town and his own house is a prophet without honour". Maybe that is the reason why the NFO crew regularly leave their company's base and present results at their clients' premises. That, of course, is only meant in jest.

9.2 Pairing-up time at ISIS

Since 2001 at ISIS, each of the large customers has been looked after by just two staff members: a Key Account Manager and a Customer Project Manager. There are different pairs for the different industries - e.g. one for large companies, one for the public sector and one for carrier companies. Less is more, as the expression goes, and these two ISIS colleagues take their duties very seriously.

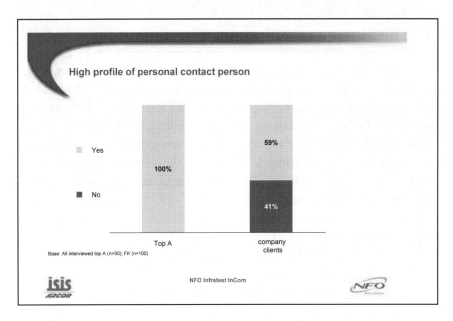

Fig. 2: High profile of personal contact person

After all, simply waiting for customers to complain and then reacting is not a sensible policy. Rather, what is needed is to look after customers in active ways, arranging visits, offering product presentations, and documenting all contacts in minute detail. What we called our Sales Portal, a database with all the details about every visit, the preferences and dislikes of the customer, amongst much besides, has since then been helping with the preparation and subsequent processing of every meeting and also guarantees that any presents given as thank-yous on this or that opportunity will be fully appreciated. In time, a detailed history of customer contacts is built up, including their purpose, those present, the measures taken, and any positive or negative effects arising there from. Evaluation of this database provides a great deal of useful guidance about dealing with our clients. And they thank us for this care - overall, the termination quota fell by half in 2002 and not one of the several hundred top-business customers turned its back on us.

9.3   The higher you climb, the further you have to fall

Our current problem is the following: how can we maintain our successful customer retention record at this high level? NFO advises against yet stronger measures, since a TRI*M index of 90 cannot realistically be improved upon. For this reason, our modus operandi is now to use this solid base to sell enhancing products and further new products to the customers. Here, too, the survey has useful help to offer. All who work at ISIS have been energetic in keeping customers informed; they have carried out workshops, initiated mailings and given consultations. Nevertheless, time and again, a disappointing conclusion from all these contact efforts is that our customers know too little about our range of services. And what they know nothing about, they cannot buy. The NFO study rescued us from a state of fumbling helplessness by graphically highlighting our dilemma with stark brutality. A black "warning triangle" - about a situation which shows signs of worsening further - is metaphorically standing in our way. It tells us that "information about new products and the service range of ISIS" is assessed as being "far below average".

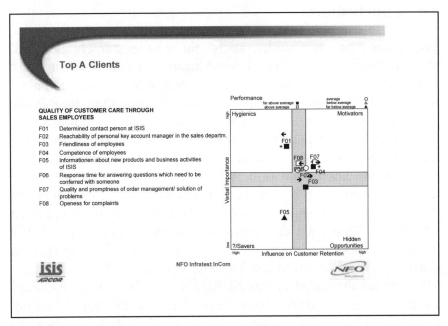

Fig. 3: Top A clients

Now everyone at ISIS is convinced of this truth and we have formulated the first creative ideas about how we can arouse stronger interest in our product diversity. Such ideas are usually generated in the working groups brought into being after every NFO report. For instance, we are now able to redress the problem that many private customers did not find our invoices sufficiently clear. The Billing Working Group drew up a formulation for invoices that is now acceptable to everyone. This success was contributed by tests whereby the occasional invoice was shown by staff members to their grandmothers - although that does not mean that invoices could not be made simpler for young people as well. As a consequence of the latest satisfaction survey, we have established 10 new Working Groups in order, among other things, to optimise letters to customers and to make our forms clearer.

9.4 Conclusions

Two years ago, we hardly knew our best customers and had identified only a few proper contact people. If one of them had a problem with our products, we were at best able to react hesitantly. If the customer cancelled his contract, all too often we simply allowed it to happen. Today 100 percent of our big business customers know their personal contact at ISIS and if we learn of the mere intention to cancel a contract, this individual contacts the right person in the unsatisfied firm. What we have managed to achieve with this group of top business customers will also succeed with the medium-sized and small businesses. Suitable customer retention instruments have been developed and are being implemented. We therefore expect no less from the forthcoming NFO survey than confirmation of further successes. The first signs of contact intensification are that contract cancellations during 2002 in the medium-sized customer segment have been reduced by our Customer Retention Team by two-thirds. This team has existed since the presentation of the shameful results from the NFO study in 2000.

Further highlights

Also improved compared with the survey conducted in 2001 is the reaction time and reliability of ISIS employees following enquiries by customers. "Rapid competent responses" and "holding to deadlines" have been expressly identified by those questioned, although a certain amount of criticism is still being voiced concerning information about the progress of order processing. ISIS is placing greater emphasis on information processing, along with some other points which are being specifically targeted by task forces of suitable specialists.

Fig. 4: Further highlights

Something that is particularly pleasing for both sides - the customers and the company itself - is that ISIS is regarded as a fair-minded and technically competent partner with whom a long-term business relationship can be formed. 100% of the top-company customers questioned would choose ISIS again as their service provider and as many recommend ISIS to others. The company has now earned a reputation as a classical high quality provider developing individual solutions in the fields of telephone, internet, dedicated connections and security, among other things. The internet/data transmission sector enjoys a high regard among customers; even the clarity of costs and tariffs is assessed positively - something that is not particularly widespread in the telecommunications industry. In this respect the innovative potential of ISIS is as clearly evident as the competence of its customer care.

Fig. 5: Customer retention is a team task at ISIS

10 The Staff Survey as a Tool for Business Development

Andre Kremser

When first approaching the topic of staff surveys, it is difficult to grasp the size and complexity of such a project, since the many consequences, interactions and side-effects resulting from this type of intervention in a business are enormous. The activities and the process steps in the preparation of a staff survey are relatively easily structured. However, in the implementation phase, a dynamic is released that is able to spur a business into movement in many different ways. This was the case at the Baden-Württembergische Bank AG, Stuttgart (BW-Bank for short). A survey of all the bank's staff was carried out for the first time in 2000.

This article describes the survey in detail, dividing the procedure into four phases corresponding to the actual chronological sequence:

1. Preparation
2. Implementation and evaluation
3. Communication of results
4. Follow-up process

The main focus is placed on the "pressure points", which in a project of this kind can also turn out to be "sticking points".

Baden-Württembergische Bank AG

Baden-Württembergische Bank AG is the largest privately-owned commercial bank in Baden-Württemberg and specialises in small and medium-sized business customers as well as high net-worth private customers. Its predecessors are the central banks of the state – Badische Bank and Württembergische Bank – and the Handelsbank Heilbronn, which all merged in 1977.

BW-Bank has its headquarters in Stuttgart and, with 53 branches, has a widespread presence throughout the south-east of Germany, as well as in Dresden, Leipzig and Halle, on Guernsey and in Hong Kong. In Frankfurt, the Bank has a stock exchange department. It also has three foreign daughter companies in Zürich, Dublin and New York.

In addition to its traditional strengths in the commercial sector, BW-Bank is developing its investment banking arm. It is taking a leading position with stock market flotations in Baden-Württemberg and looks after numerous clients in its Mergers & Acquisitions division, many of them together with its investment banking subsidiary, BW Capital Markets. For its export-oriented small and medium-sized customers, BW-Bank is an experienced partner in all their foreign activities.

Client investments in the group up to 31st December 2002 totalled 12.5 billion Euro and, with total assets of 26.1 billion Euro, the group achieved a turnover of 27.3 billion Euro.

10.1 Preparation

When a survey of this type is to be undertaken for the first time, careful preparation is of the utmost importance. One cannot be too conscientious in this phase; every error and carelessness in preparation may have a negative effect during the course of the process, with the consequence that the staff and/or the management fail to support the survey and the follow-up process to the extent required. That is why the entire project sequence must be precisely planned in every detail before the survey begins; so it is important that all those involved in the project are aware of their roles and responsibilities.

10.1.1 The participants

A variety of persons and groups were involved in the different phases of the project.

An **internal project team** of 3 people from the Personnel Department of BW-Bank initiated the staff survey and took responsibility for following through the entire project. I was a member of this project group.

In addition, two external partner organisations were involved in the project. For the conception of the questionnaire form, we had the support of the management consultants **Unternehmensberatung STRATA GmbH**. Evaluation of the survey was carried out by **NFO Infratest Wirtschaftsforschung**, who also gave valuable help with the results tools.

In our experience, it is advisable and – depending on the type of survey – even required under German labour relations law to involve the **staff council members** in the project as employee representatives. When a survey of this type is carried out for the first time, it can lead to scepticism among individual employees or employee groups concerning the seriousness or confidentiality of the procedure. Getting the staff council involved at this stage can therefore help to build confidence.

The most important people in the procedure, finally, are the **employees and management of the bank**. An employee survey lives or dies with the involvement of the target group. Many employees will also have undertaken a pre-test in focus groups and, in the implementation phase, participated in follow-up teams, as explained below.

If that section of the staff that constitutes the **management** is given particular emphasis, then it is because they have to be the motor for change. Without their driving force, no employee survey can produce positive results.

10.1.2 The questionnaire form

The questionnaire form is of decisive importance to the success of such an undertaking and there are three criteria that warrant particular attention: the number of questions, the choice of questions and the statistical data. I will now deal with these factors in greater detail.

It was important for the project group to obtain a comprehensive view of the bank from the employees' viewpoint, particularly in the first survey. Based on this goal, a questionnaire form with some 130 items was developed in conjunction with the consultants from STRATA Unternehmensberatung, covering the following areas:

1. Image and ethos of BW-Bank
2. Customer-orientation and service quality
3. Personal work situation
4. Organisation of work
5. Information and communication
6. Leadership behaviour
7. Career development opportunities
8. Pay and supplementary benefits

The questionnaire form was tested in the context of a pre-test involving about 60 employees from different business sectors and hierarchical levels. This test provided valuable information about which items were difficult to understand or could be misinterpreted. Afterwards, the questionnaire form was revised accordingly.

It is self-evidently true that the more extensive the questionnaire is – and therefore the more time it takes to fill in – the smaller will be the response rate. A questionnaire with 130 items is extensive. We took the view, however, that a resultant response loss could be avoided by suitable marketing measures.

But in this regard we were in error. We are now firmly convinced that a questionnaire of this type should not contain more than 80 items; not only because of the response rate, but also on account of the processing workload during the follow-up procedure.

The choice of questions is also of decisive importance to the success of an employee survey, since the survey itself generates expectations of change among the staff. Those subject areas that are regarded and experienced critically by the employees should be dealt with and improved following a survey of this type. It should therefore only contain questions about things that can be changed afterwards and which the management is allowed to change. Otherwise the result will be disappointed expectations, which disrupt the follow-up process and impede subsequent surveys.

In order to evaluate a staff survey in differentiated fashion, statistical information must be available. For that reason, two statistical items are dealt with at the end of the form: the organisational position and leadership responsibilities.

The question relating to organisational unit (branch, department, group etc.) is important not only to be able to evaluate results for BW-Bank as a whole, but also for the individual units. For this purpose, the structural organisation was broken down into units of at least 6 persons. For reasons of anonymity, we dispensed with smaller groups. Staff members had only to put a cross by the description of their organisational unit.

The leadership responsibility question was important to us to learn whether employee satisfaction and company loyalty differ significantly between those with and those without leadership responsibility.

At this point, I would like to deal briefly with the subject of **anonymity**, since apart from the scope of a questionnaire, an assurance of anonymity is also a decisive criterion in determining response rate.

We would have liked to incorporate further differentiating features, such as gender and length of service. Whether these further differentiating factors would indeed have made significant differences apparent, we do not know. That notwithstanding, all statistical interests must remain subordinate to anonymity. And not only objective anonymity, but the subjectively perceived anonymity of the target group. In this regard, we had to do a great deal of persuading work during the survey, since although the two statistical features were not linked during evaluation, individual leaders had reservations in this regard. This is also understandable, particularly since small organisational units have only one leader and this person would be identified if they filled in the questionnaire form and answered the statistical questions regarding "organisational unit" and "leadership responsibility".

"Six" was the magic number for evaluating the results. Only when there were six questionnaire forms with identical statistical information was a group evaluation carried out for these, provided the results of the survey were statistically stable.

10.1.3 Announcing the survey

Four weeks before the survey, we sent flyers to all the employees announcing the survey itself, describing the process and giving an overview of the further activities. In parallel with this and from this point on, we published up-to-date information in every issue of our quarterly staff journal *Aspekte*. Information was also drawn up, posted, and constantly updated on the intranet.

10.2 Carrying out and evaluating the survey

The survey itself is the simplest part, looking at the project overall. The activities of the project team concentrated, during this phase, on marketing with the aim of achieving a high response rate. That aim is only realistic if the survey is both simple to carry out and interesting for the target group.

Marketing began with the questionnaire form itself. The layout was professionally designed at an advertising agency. On the cover sheet was a photograph with domino blocks standing upright, the first of them being just about to fall over (producing the domino effect). This image was intended to symbolise the impetus to change, which also inspired the title of the form: "Provide the impetus". The domino image served as the symbol of the survey throughout the project.

Every employee was given a questionnaire form in a sealed envelope. Also enclosed was a letter from the chairman with, stuck onto the top right hand corner, a wooden domino, and the data protection declaration from NFO Infratest Wirtschaftsforschung. Two address labels were also included – one with the internal house post address for the project group and another with the postal address of NFO Infratest in Munich. Each employee was thus free to choose whether to send the form to Infratest or to us. We collected the forms addressed to us and passed all of them together to NFO Infratest.

The period set for answering the questionnaire was 4 weeks. After two weeks, every employee was sent a reminder, requesting them to participate in the survey. After expiry of the stated period, we allowed an extra 2 weeks for late posting. During the survey period, there was a telephone hotline to the project group for any questions regarding the form.

We then only had a small window of time for the evaluation and communication of the results. Because of the timing of the holidays, the survey could only be conducted after the 2000 summer holiday period and communication of the results had to be largely completed before the start of the year-end business – that is, by the end of November. That meant that Infratest had to determine the results of the survey under intense pressure.

10.3 Communicating the results

Despite intensive efforts to achieve a high participation quota – including offering a prize – we did not succeed in passing the magical 50% mark. In the end, the response rate for the whole bank was 48%, whereby the quotas in the individual organisational units varied greatly. In the sectors in which the response rate did not provide a stable result, no individual results were achieved. The answers from these forms were assigned to the next highest organisational unit.

For our purposes, the response rate was unsatisfactory and we attribute this to two factors: the scope of the questionnaire form, mentioned above, and a degree of fear among employees who lacked experience of this instrument. During the further course of the project, many employees of both genders admitted their fears regarding anonymity to us. However, a great deal of trust was built up by the representation of the results and the evaluation tools from NFO Infratest. This was repeatedly confirmed to us and has provided encourage-ment for further projects of this type.

The results of the survey were determined for the whole bank, for the divisions (Corporate and Private Customer business) and for the respective organisational units. The Management Board, the heads of the second leadership level and the whole central staff council were presented with the results for the bank overall. The results were also published in a brochure which was given to all the staff.

In addition, the results for each respective organisational unit were presented to all staff members and leaders in the context of presentations of the results for each organisational unit. These presentations were undertaken partly by NFO Infratest itself and partly by the consultants of STRATA Unternehmensberatung together with a member of the project team.

In order to avoid competitive thinking, no results from other sectors were published. Only aggregate data or an anonymous benchmark were used for comparative purposes. We were clear that the individual results would be passed on by word of mouth among the employees. This is not an unusual process; rather it is the rule, but we did not want to encourage such informal exchanges.

10.4 The follow-up process

10.4.1 Basic considerations on the implementation process

A staff survey is basically a conveying means by which systematic guidance points for the strengths and weaknesses of an organisation may be obtained. Knowledge of the strengths and weaknesses alone is not sufficient; the aim is to obtain stronger staff loyalty by means of a lasting improvement in working conditions. The real work begins when the results have been gathered in.

It is therefore of essential importance to design the implementation process target-oriented. In our experience, three factors are decisive:

Solutions rather than problems

Where the survey yielded critical responses, the respective leadership figures had a special interest in discovering the origins of these criticisms. This is understandable, although in our experience, discussions in this direction do not lead very far, since employees resist when asked to explain their answers to the questionnaire retrospectively. This erodes anonymity, on which staff place a particular value, especially when their answers are critical. Added to this is the fact that even analysing the causes of an unsatisfactory situation in a profound manner does not always bring an improvement any closer. It is therefore meaningful in our view to start thinking straight away about what can be done in order to improve critical situations. In this way, no one is responsible for a problem, but everyone is responsible for the solution. In order to avoid misunderstandings, our intention is not to "sweep problems under the rug". But, in our experience the search for causes has a negative influence on the debate and tends to oppress those who participate.

Only concrete measures lead to improvements

A small example to begin with. Let us assume that in a staff survey, the criticism arose that managers decide too much and employees are given too little responsibility. How could an improvement measure be formulated?

- In future, managers will pass more responsibility to their employees
  or
- From next month, employees may themselves clear invoices up to a volume of 20,000 Euro per month. In about 6 months, on (date), we will examine our experience of this measure in our team discussion.

The question of which improvement measure has the greater chances of success is superfluous.

Planned measures only lead to lasting improvements if
- they are formulated in concrete terms,
- the responsibilities (and persons) are clearly established,
- deadlines are clearly defined,
- and monitored

These are "classical" requirements. Although they sound simple, sometimes they are difficult to implement. What is required is openness and clarity from all involved in discussions, as well as commitment when taking action.

Less is more

This point is easily dealt with: it is usually more successful to undertake a few improvement measures and to see them through consistently than to take many measures that are not seen through to completion, creating an impression of unthinking activity. It is not the number of activities that brings about greater employee satisfaction, but the effectiveness and permanence of the improvement measures.

10.4.2 The follow-up teams

Communication of the results released a good deal of dynamic impetus in the bank, which found expression in numerous discussions and talks about the results. This is due, above all, to the fact that some of the results differed greatly between different departments. One thing this survey showed very clearly is that there is not only one company culture, but a multiplicity of company cultures within our organisation. These cultures are primarily mar-ked by the tasks and functions of the individual departments, the leadership situation and by regional differences in mentality.

Our task now as the project group was to utilise the energy of the numerous discussions towards lasting change processes. We therefore defined suitable structures and processes for the further continuation of the project.

For the follow-up process, follow-up teams (or FUP teams) were formed. Each of these contained between 4 and 10 people and their composition was chosen to be representative of their organisational unit. The teams also included the respective leader, a local staff council member and the Quality Representative[1]. These teams were constituted in this manner because it was only sensible and practicable to involve all the organisation members in the process if they were in small organisational units (up to 12 persons).

---

[1] There is a Quality Representative in every organisational unit of the bank. This person is responsible for ensuring that complaints from external or internal clients are systematically recorded and processed. Through the blanket coverage provided by the Quality Representatives and the systematic processing of complaints, it is possible in particular to discover and rectify structural weaknesses in the organisation.

The teams worked out concrete improvement measures in the context of guided discussions, with the guiding being undertaken by individual team members who had been suitably trained before the survey. In difficult discussion situations, members of the project group were also brought in. The results of the discussions were continuously communicated to the respective operational units. Some of the teams were highly creative in designing the process. For instance, the FUP team for the main branch in Freiburg organised a whole group event at which almost 100 employees expressed their ideas for improvement measures. These ideas were then converted into concrete measures by the FUP team.

Fig. 1: The follow-up team for the Freiburg main branch during preparations for the whole group event (Fig. 3)

Fig. 2: The follow-up team for the Freiburg main branch during preparations for the whole group event (Fig. 3)

It was possible to process about 80% of the criticisms within the respective organisational units and bring about improvements with suitable measures. In the remaining cases, the problem lay in the co-operation of two or more organisational areas and improvement measures could therefore only be implemented in cooperation with these departments. In those cases, it was the respective Quality Representatives in the relevant FUP teams who acted as a contact point and organised joint discussions among the teams. This procedure was extremely successful.

The improvement measures worked out were recorded in writing and the results were reported once a month by the project team to the management. This arrangement proved to be disadvantageous since, as the project group, we found ourselves assuming conflicting roles. On the one hand, we were supporters for the follow-up teams in all questions regarding the implementation process, whereby we often received a very deep and often confidential insight into the inner life of the organisation. On the other hand, we also received or demanded the results reports and were therefore also the controllers of the process with close contact to the management. This meant that, to a certain extent, we had taken on a classical leadership role. These two roles are not necessarily mutually exclusive, although they hinder each other in some situations. In retrospect, we would recommend a clear separation. Control of the process must rest in the hands of the next higher superior and the project team should concentrate on its task as the process adviser.

A further word on the role of the leadership.

Change processes will succeed or fail dependent upon the leadership's commitment to – and level of identification with – the changes worked out. The success of the follow-up process subsequent to a staff survey also heavily depends upon this. It is therefore absolutely necessary that all leaders – from the management board to group leaders – are convinced of the sense and necessity of the project. The staff of an organisation sense very acutely whether their superiors take the process seriously or not. All leaders must therefore be "sworn in". So as to underline the significance of the implementation process, this was made part of the target agreements of the leaders and therefore also influenced their pay. This measure may emphasise the importance of the implementation process, though not necessarily generate awareness of it. And if that is lacking, leaders do not become the drivers of the follow-up process, but are merely driven by their target agreements. This can have disastrous consequences, since employees react angrily or stubbornly if they notice that the activities initiated do not (or are not intended to) lead to real improvements in their working conditions, but only serve as a pretence to secure the income of their superiors. In a few cases, we needed to intercede in our capacity as the project group.

10.4.3 Examples of concrete measures

The change measures arising from the results of the staff survey were similar in many areas, though overall they were highly diverse and had differing consequences. Here are some examples:

- In many areas regular discussions have been introduced to improve the information flow. In other organisational units, the already regularly held discussions were optimised.
- In the Mannheim main branch, at the employees' request, a canteen that had been closed for a number of years was re-opened.
- In the Leipzig main branch, a new works agreement about flexible working hours was concluded.
- In the Stuttgart main branch, a job rotation program was developed and implemented, whereby the staff dealing with customers and back-office workers swapped places for a limited time. This means that staff groups learn more about each other's work and develop greater mutual understanding. Precisely this was often lacking in their work together and led to cooperative dysfunctionalities.
- Critical results concerning the leadership environment have led, in individual cases, to staffing changes.
- A lack of contact with the management criticised in the survey was tackled with a question-and-answer forum on the internet and "lunch with the board". The latter, after a hesitant take-up at first, has since grown in popularity. Every employee can go to lunch with every member of the management board. A brief e-mail suffices and a date is then agreed.

Numerous measures have been published in an Ideas Factory on the Internet if they are not of interest solely to the department that produced them. In this way, we have publicised activities arising from the follow-up process of the staff survey and simultaneously provided for a cross-disciplinary exchange of ideas between organisational units. We are, as ever, of the view that this is a good starting point, even publication of individual improvement measures has been interpreted as "running for benchmarks". Something that has been publicised as progress for one operational unit may be nothing special for another. As the project group, we had to point out repeatedly that the object was "only" to increase work satisfaction in one's own department and not to be better than others.

Summary and prospects

The staff survey was not an isolated measure for improving structures and processes. After all, complaints management and customer surveys have the same aim. Those responsible within the project for these different instruments therefore met regularly and exchanged views. This networking enhanced the significance of the individual measures. In my own view, it is therefore no exaggeration to describe a staff survey as an instrument for business development.

Fig. 3: Those responsible within the project for complaint management, the staff survey and the customer survey (from l to r: Falkinger, Kremser, Fellhauer, Morlock)

I am convinced that three personal qualities are decisive for the success of a staff survey: courage, determination and endurance.

- Courage is necessary because the decision for a staff survey begins a process whose outcome is unknown and which changes an organisation at many points and in many ways. Those changes are not predictable in advance
- Determination is required so as not to become stuck half way, and in order to see through the changes worked out as part of the implementation process
- Endurance is needed because one thing must not be overlooked: in the course of a process like this, there are always difficulties and set-backs. It would be regrettable if those involved were then to withdraw (saying "it will never work anyway"). And set-backs offer valuable information about why something fails to work – information that, in turn, makes it easier to seek new solutions.

As the project group, we too learned a great deal about staff surveys as an instrument and about its effects in an organisation. We also learned from the mistakes we made. This experience will be put to good use in follow-on surveys[2] and other comparable interventions.

And another thing. As any master craftsman can confirm, good tools are vital to achieving good results. The same applies here. The extensive evaluation tools and differential analyses used by NFO Infratest Wirtschaftsforschung were and are the basis for a project of this type. Such a project should not be undertaken without such well-established instruments.

---

[2] Due to major changes within the group, a planned follow-on survey has had to be postponed.

11 The Employee Survey as a Milestone in Business Development

Wolfgang Werner

11.1 The starting position

Degussa is a chemicals group with roughly 50,000 employees, an annual turnover of 11.756 billion Euros (for 2002) and was formed in February 2001 with the merger of VEBA and VIAG. The main participating parties, SKW Trostberg and Degussa-Hüls, were themselves the result of recent mergers or takeovers. The chemical companies involved are shown in fig. 1.

They are, without exception, renowned companies within the industry, some of them with a long tradition and highly developed cultures of their own.

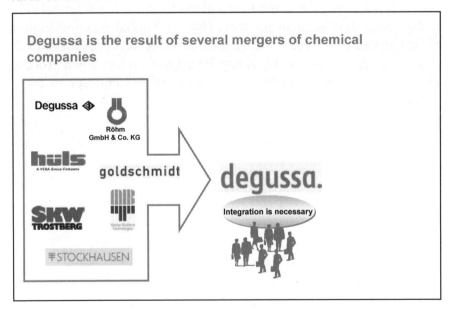

Fig. 1: Merger

Strategic restructuring involving reorientation into a highly focused specialty chemicals business was executed rapidly and accompanied by a portfolio tidy up and the acquisition of suitable companies, such as Laporte plc.

The simultaneous development of a new Degussa identity, within the group, was unable to meet the fast pace of fusion.

The culture development process thus began.

From the very start it was clear – as in many fusion processes – that cultural differences between the companies would require special attention. In particular, the fact that the employees of the new Degussa were coming from highly successful companies with long traditions of their own, made for identification with the new group quite difficult. A shared identity was necessary for strategic reasons. The position of the group in the market and in the estimation of the capital markets would be strengthened by the development of this identity, enabling synergy effects between the various parts of the group to take place. The end result would create added value for the customers and employees alike.

The establishment of a unified corporate vision played a central role in the group development proccess (fig. 2). Global communication of the corporate concept led to the manifestation and implementation of the Vision, Mission and Guiding Principles – a top-down process whose aim was to promote a realization of this concept in daily work.

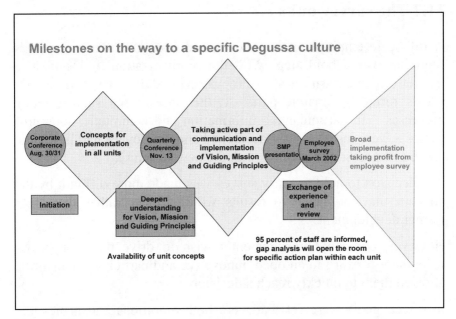

Fig. 2: The Corporate Development Process

It was communicated clearly from the beginning that this process would not continue "on autopilot", but instead the first results would be investigated by means of an employee survey. Implementation would be directly monitored so that the tendency towards generating biased reports with positive results and problems with regular reporting would be eliminated. Indirect monitoring through questioning those involved parties has important aspects, which affect the development process:

- Inclusion of all employees and a measurement of the direct effects on individuals

- Emphasis setting; indirectly communicating the most important topics by means of a targeted question selection

- Monitoring information; regular information on the state of organizational development

This article does not apply to other cultural development process measures or activities included in "Blue Spirit"; it deals exclusively with employee surveys.

11.2 The survey units

A full-scale employee survey conducted one year after the group's founding was a bold step. With the reorganization of Degussa, a market-oriented business structure was created that extended directly across formerly separate parts. At the time of the survey, many processes – in particular the information and communications processes – were insufficiently developed and employees had little time and limited reason to identify with the new structure.

The decision to hold an early survey was made more difficult by the concern that too negative results would hinder rather than help further development.

However, company management's wish to drive the group's development forward in an open, innovative and participatory manner, allowed them to quickly reach a decision.

In effect, goals were set that were both ambitious and achievable (fig. 3):

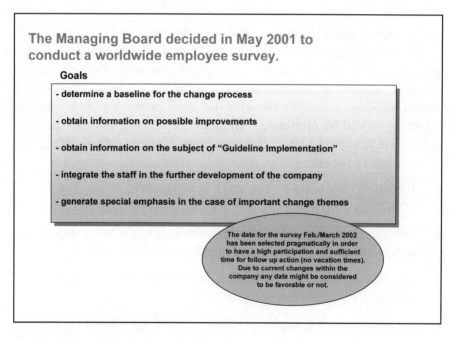

The Managing Board decided in May 2001 to conduct a worldwide employee survey.

Goals

- determine a baseline for the change process

- obtain information on possible improvements

- obtain information on the subject of "Guideline Implementation"

- integrate the staff in the further development of the company

- generate special emphasis in the case of important change themes

The date for the survey Feb./March 2002 has been selected pragmatically in order to have a high participation and sufficient time for follow up action (no vacation times). Due to current changes within the company any date might be considered to be favorable or not.

Fig. 3: Aims of the survey

Looking at the historical development of the various parts of the group, it was decided that due to the frequent fusions and takeovers, any employee identification with the holding company would be low. It was assumed that employees identify most with their environment, such as their own site/workplace. Therefore, when designing the questionnaire, value was placed on testing this thesis. As a second point of emphasis, a familiarity with and an acceptance of the new corporate image was also put to the test.

Furthermore, the questionnaire contained the typical topics of a comprehensive staff survey, such as work satisfaction, leadership, development possibilities, etc. fig. 4 gives a comprehensive overview of these.

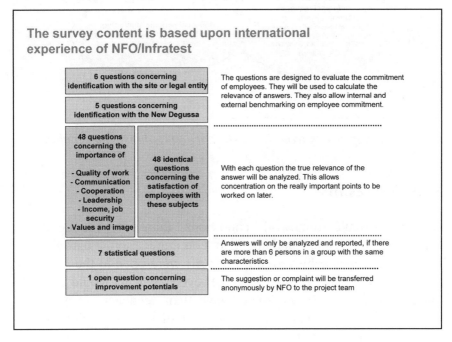

Fig. 4: Questionnaire contents

The logistic aspects of the survey represented a particular challenge. Six months after the group's founding, staffing lists, local structures and communication structures had to be in place to allow the preparation of communications and document distribution. In one Herculean effort, all this was achieved in time; the complexity of the task is illustrated by some key figures:

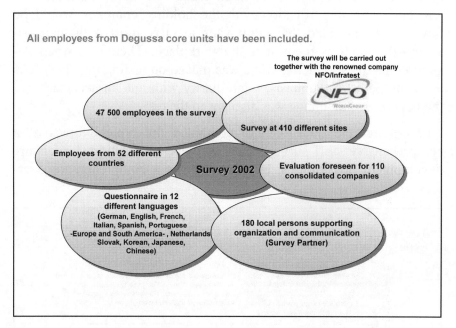

Fig. 5: All employees from Degussa core units have been included

11.3 The results

Despite difficult framework conditions, thanks to the dedicated commitment of leaders and abundant communication, a participation level of 62% was achieved. 88% of staff were open to the notion of an employee survey and 60% believed that it would lead to improvements. 6,700 employees gave their feedback, in a section intended for additional comments, to indicate faults and opportunities for improvement.

Initially, the evaluation yielded the expected pattern. Calculated from the first six survey questions, the commitment of staff members to their familiar surroundings is roughly average. When compared to the new Degussa, it is all of 6 index points lower. It is clear, from fig. 6, that there are also large regional differences. There was a general problem with the international acceptance of a company that in the past was strongly focused on only Germany. There are restructuring problems in some countries, although these will not be considered here.

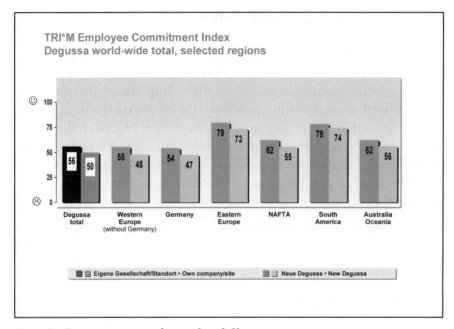

Fig. 6: Commitment indexes for different regions

Alongside the Employee Commitment Index, the evaluation tools utilized were Employee Typology and the TRI*M Grid from NFO. The typologies revealed that the percentage of employees not reached was above average. An alarming factor in this regard was the small difference in the typology for leaders and remaining employees. This discovery has led to special measures being developed at the corporate level for leadership development.

The TRI*M Grids first provided department-specific, concrete indications of where the need for improvements lie. These include the "typical topics" of staff surveys: high levels of satisfaction with one's immediate working environment, colleagues, safety at work; average satisfaction with superiors and levels of compensation; dissatisfaction with communication, involvement and opportunities for further development.

On aggregate, it was found that among other things, the values firmly established within the structures of business leadership are either not well known or are not always perceived positively in daily life.

11.4 The implementation phase

A specially instructed and trained group of some 250 survey coaches interpreted and explained all results disclosed to the company's leaders. While paying attention to the group policy of the most decentralized responsibility possible, the processing of improvement issues and their implementation were then placed in the hands of the leaders. Of the group management, the leaders of the larger organizational units were asked only to state what they saw as being the three most important points. The result of this process is shown in fig. 7.

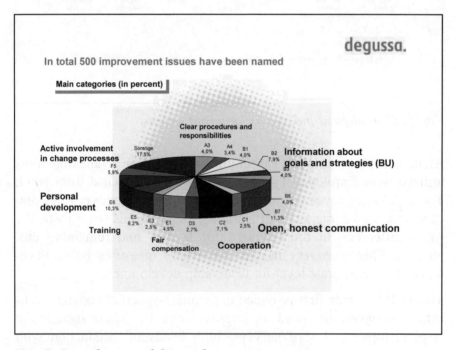

Fig. 7: Distribution of the implementation measures

Many of these topics for improvement and other priorities were taken on in workshops with the cooperation of employees. The fact that open and honest communication is the most frequently cited problem area is probably connected to the unique company situation. Fusion phases and subsequent porfolio measures are frequently characterized by hesitant communication, either because information that comes too early can hinder planning or, for reasons of uncertainty, no information is forthcoming.

Implementation of the measures stipulated is controlled by the respective leader, usually in project teams. A great deal of value has been placed on results, failures and also successes being reported on an up-to-date basis. Improvements have often taken place which are not recognized as being connected to the staff survey. Employee attention should be focussed on continuing the improvement process.

Communication often existed by means of internal publications, employee newspapers or special leaflets. It was then that the first differences resulting from the implementation of feedback were noticeable.

In parallel with these decentralized activities, it was established that there was a need for action at the highest group level and these issues were tackled with projects and special measures. Examples of this are heightened efforts made in the direction of transparent communication and measures taken in the area of leadership development.

11.5 Monitoring

According to the principle that no direct project monitoring was to be conducted, but rather that the effects of measures on employees were to be gauged, six months after the initial survey an "after-survey" was initiated. This was carried out online with a short questionnaire for those with an internet connection. The staff members were selected at random and the survey was initially carried out only in Germany and the USA in order to gather experience with the online method.

The results showed that communication of the group survey results had functioned extremely well. However, there were differences in the communication with departmental results, as expected, and these provided the impetus for targeted questionnaires among the respective leaders.

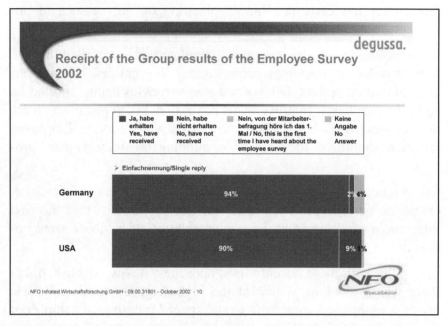

Fig. 8: Results of the online questionnaire, communication

Not enough time was calculated prior to the distribution of the full survey to measure the effects of the first improvements made. Nevertheless, only 13% of the staff were of the opinion that no work was being done on improvements, 55% had a positive impression and 30% were uncertain.

In the course of a second random sample questionnaire conducted a year later, measuring the Employee Commitment Index was yet again hazard. Considering the acceptance of the new "Degussa" identity was of interest, the measurement of site commitment was no longer pursued. The survey was carried out in mixed format with online and written questionnaires in order to enable employees without internet access – in particular the staff members in fully continuous production plants – to express their opinions. The results yielded dense information, which when organized in a new form, provided control information.

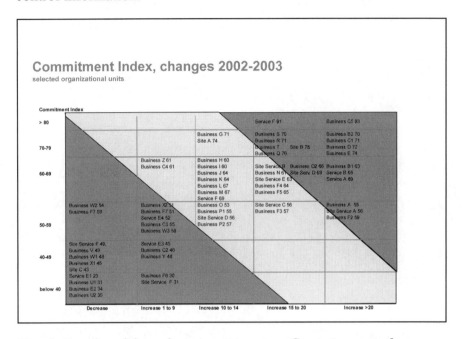

Fig. 9: Results of the online questionnaire; Commitment index change

(Departmental designations are neutralised)

It is clearly evident that there is a correlation between the size of the index and the index increase within a year. Without overinterpreting the results, clear effects may be seen from local measures (e.g. restructuring) or specific leadership behaviour.

The random sample questionnaires will be continued until the next full survey, in order to obtain further control information for the business development process. In the business development process, the topic of a targeted contribution to the HR strategy of the company needs to be continuously considered.

. . . .
. . . .
. . . .
. . . .

12 Building a Customer-Centric Culture

Sanjeev Luther

The M&T's over-arching business plan is to build long-term relationships with both its customers and the communities in which it
markets, leading to M&T's marketplace goal: to be the primary bank
of choice. The bedrock upon which these long-term relationships is
built is on a rock-solid foundation of highly satisfied/dedicated
employees.

The execution of the long-term plan begins, and continues, by pry-
ing open the employee's mind and examining his/her view about
what we call our "Internal" services.

> The "Internal" is the employee's perception of the quality of
> service that they are able to deliver to customers based on M&T's
> *own* ability to deliver service. If the employee is dissatisfied with
> and hamstrung by internal service providers, is there a moment's
> doubt that that annoyance/frustration will ultimately be communi-
> cated to the customer in both subtle and in overt ways?

> The prying into employee's feelings is achieved through feedback
> mechanisms (on-going employee surveys..."employee commit-
> ment survey") among those who deliver service to the customer
> (are they satisfied with the internal supplier?) and how the service
> is delivered. This feedback, in turn, lead to an Internal Service
> Excellence program which ultimately lead to specific initiatives:

> - Expanded access to extensive employee training programs.
>
> - Flexible work arrangements.
>
> - Employee suggestion program - many ideas submitted, se-
>   veral adopted and rewarded.

- Employee stock purchase program - more than a fourth have participated.

- New annual review process.

Therefore, M&T has institutionalized a feedback loop to inform management of employee's overall mind-state and the specific elements that are either plaguing or are enhancing the employee's ability to perform customer service at the level necessary to engender a long-term relationship.

"Know Thou Self " is fine, but knowing "How Others Know Us" is at a higher demand level. Yes, while we drive to achieve maximum employee satisfaction, we need periodic reality checks to assure ourselves that we are on the right road. And those "sign posts" are what we call our "External" measurements.

The "External" focus is measuring how the Customer views his/her relationship with the Bank at every touch point, market-by-market and branch-by-branch. And, most importantly, we benchmark against how our competitors feel about their bank.

TRI*M is the tool of choice for assessment. But TRI*M tells us more than just simply "how M&T appears to the world".

It is our touchstone to ensure that we are directing our finite resources on the drivers of retention. How am I performing on the critical hooks that my customers look towards in creating a level of contentment/enthusiasm that will shield them against competitor's talons?

- That competitively, we are able to identify the drivers of retention that our competitors have not latched on to or on which they are performing poorly. A major aspect of TRI*M is an exa-mination of how competitors rate their bank.

- To identify the "table stakes" (the elements I must deliver) to be in the banking game. We don't build customer loyalty on these elements. We can only lose loyalty on them if we fail to deliver.

- To spot where we might invest less heavily or worry less because it is **not** a critical area for driving the business. In which specific branches do our customers tell us we have fallen out of bed... and, not only which specific elements are causing us to fail overall, but within those problematic branches, on which aspects are they performing *relatively* well, so we can present to our managers a more balanced story. Similarly, on our top per-forming branches, we need to know relatively speaking, where is there room for improvement i.e., which element(s) is not as highly considered as others. We need the latter message to keep these better branches from becoming complacent.

Beginning in 2004, TRI*M will become one of the prime components of branch manager's bonus allocation system.

Today, each branch manager receives a periodic scorecard displaying his TRI*M Index scores relative to his close-in geographical area, his larger region and of course versus the entire bank. Included on the scorecard are ratings on the Motivators, Hygienics and those elements which are neither. At the corporate level, we use the TRI*M input to formulate our strategies on both Products and on operational elements. The individual branch manager, while far less able to directly impact on Product ratings (that is largely controlled at the corporate level), does have the wherewithal to significantly impact the operations aspect of his/her branch.

In summary, M&T aims to build the business from the inside out; not from the outside in. We focus on the employee to motivate him/her who in turn will focus with higher motivation on the customer; rather then focussing on the customer and ignoring or showing indifference to the employee and hoping for the best. Since the customer is the only one who can ultimately tell us if we are doing are job right, TRI*M has thus become our ultimate bearer of the truth of our practices.

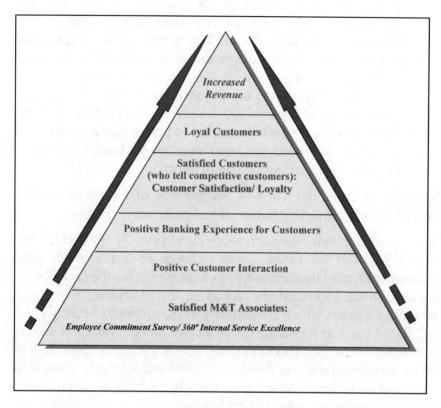

Fig. 1: This is how we envision our paradigm

13 The Balanced Scorecard as an Internal Auditing Tool

Joachim Scharioth, Margit Huber, Ian Jarvis

13.1 Practical applications of the Balanced Scorecard

13.1.1 The competitive environment

The competitive environment in which a company operates has changed radically since the 1980s. At that time product quality and the rate of product innovation were the key to achieving competitive advantage. Nowadays even a substantial product innovation often only guarantees a competitive edge for no more than 6 months or so before the competition replicates it – or even improves upon it. This does not mean that product innovation can be ignored – quite the opposite – but merely that the odds of achieving a medium-term competitive advantage by product innovation alone are becoming increasingly slim.

An answer to this change in the competitive environment was provided in the 1990s by business re-engineering, whereby companies sought to improve their internal processes, either to reduce cost and/or to improve product/service delivery to the customer. There is still a need to continually improve efficiency, but this hasn't led to companies being able to achieve a sustained competitive advantage over their competition either. Every bank, every retailer, every engineering company now operates in pretty much the same way as other companies in its sector, with the result that the returns on process improvement – as with product innovation – are now no longer much more than marginal.

Stakeholder Management

This has led to a situation where Stakeholder Management has become decisive in determining whether a company is successful in the medium term or not. 'Stakeholder Management' is concerned with the management of the relationships between a company or institution and its most important 'stakeholders' – customers, employees, shareholders, etc. – relationships which must be actively managed rather than being left to drift wherever events take them. Equally important are the relationships between different departments/functions within a company and between management and staff. A company that secures a high level of commitment from its customers and maximum commitment from its employees gains a clear advantage that no competitor can threaten. Managing these relationships therefore plays a crucial rôle in determining a company's medium-term success or failure, and Stakeholder Management has consequently become a key management tool.

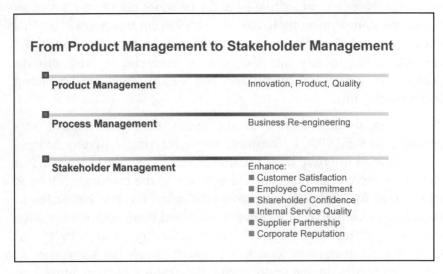

Fig. 1: From product management to stakeholder management

13.1.2 The Balanced Scorecard concept

With the Balanced Scorecard, Kaplan & Norton introduced two new ideas in the area of performance measurement and management.

Firstly, the Balanced Scorecard takes a broad view of performance measurement, not just restricted to financial measures but including also customer relationships, business processes and employee motivation (including the company's capacity for innovation, through its employees).

Secondly, it sets performance targets for each of the four areas (financials, customers, processes, employees/innovation) in relation to the company's overall vision and strategy; so that not only does each area have its own performance measures that management can monitor against targets, but progress in each area contributes to the achievement of the company's overall objectives.

Interactions between areas

These two extensions to the practice of performance measurement are very convincing, even obvious at first sight. However, less obvious is the fact that all four areas are interdependent, and that an action taken to reach an objective in one area has an impact not only in that area but in the other three as well. For example, if a company has a cost reduction target in order to improve its financial performance, other things being equal this will impact on staffing levels and consequently on staff motivation, the company's capacity to perform certain processes and on customer relations; conversely, if a company decides to implement a new broad-based marketing strategy, again other things being equal, this will impact on staff workloads (and on staff motivation and customer service levels), and on short-term financial results. The key phrase here is "other things being equal", because other things aren't equal: objectives in each area – and therefore the targets set and the actions undertaken – must take account of each other and be planned as a coherent whole.

138

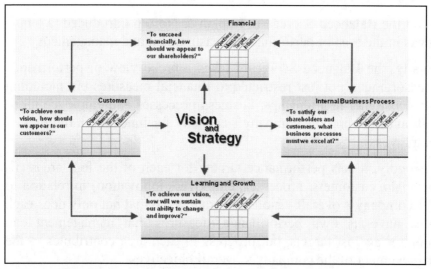

Source: Robert S. Kaplan und David P. Norton, "Using the Balanced Scorecard as a Strategic Management System"

Fig. 2: Vision and strategy

13.1.3 Balanced Scorecard operating levels

Targets and measurement

The construction of the actual Scorecard, with its detailed targets and measurements that can only be determined by top operational management together with the internal auditors, has to be carefully separated from goal setting, which can only be done by the management board as a function of corporate strategy.

Relationship between Goals, Measurement and Application

Goals   can only be set by Top Management – for the company as a whole, and for the individual business units within the company

Measure-   the measurement system must also be specified centrally so that
ment   the same measures are applied consistantly across the company, both in terms of the nature of the measures (sales, ROI, customer satisfaction, etc.) and in terms of the 'currencies' employed ($, hours/minutes, indices, etc.)

Application is the responsibility of the operational management of each business unit, ensuring that the unit-specific measures are consistent with the company-wide measurement system and that the targets set will achieve the company's overall goals

---

Fig. 3: Relationship between goals, measurement and implementation

Roles

A Balanced Scorecard only works properly if the rôles of all participants are clearly identified. The Board of Directors sets the overall corporate strategy; top operational management and the internal audit function then set the targets for each of the four areas (financials, customers, processes, employees/innovation) that will fulfil this strategy; day-to-day operational management then decides what actions need to be taken to achieve these targets, always bearing in mind that any proposed action will impact on all four areas, not just the one it is designed for.

13.1.4 The Balanced Scorecard as a strategic management tool

There are many familiar elements in the conceptual framework of the Balanced Scorecard. However, the new element is that the Balanced Scorecard gives management a single tool that provides an appropriate performance measurement system for a whole range of management strategies:

•Stakeholder Management	• The Customer-focused Organisation
•Total Quality Management	• Value-based Activity Management
•Just-in-time Production and Distribution	• Empowerment/ Entrepreneurship
•Time Management	• Risk Management
•Time for Innovation	• Re-engineering
•Lean Management	• The Learning Organisation

Fig. 4: Management strategies

Risk Management

The benefits of a Risk Management strategy are obvious, but it also specifically requires using a Balanced Scorecard type of approach. We can already see this happening as companies increasingly move away from measuring performance solely in terms of historical financial results to include also – as encouraged by auditors and, in Germany, by the KonTraG – the sort of future-oriented measures required by modern Risk Management. By considering simultaneously customer retention, employee commitment, innovation potential and process efficiency, it is possible to implement a future-oriented performance measurement system in which the various objectives are balanced one against the other. This leads to a broadening of the success factors being considered, without however abandoning the ability to focus on individual success factors or elements within them. Indeed what emerges is the desirability, even necessity, to concentrate on those central issues that bring benefits in all four areas.

Implementation using standard measures

This is only possible if measurement is genuinely implemented across the whole company. Both corporate goals and the actual performance measurements chosen have to be such that they can be broken down and applied in a comparable manner, not only at the individual business unit level within a company, but also potentially at a company level in comparison with other companies.

It is conceivable that individual business units will need to have specific performance measures appropriate to their functions/ activities, in addition to the standard company-wide measures, but in such cases these additional measures should not be included in the overall corporate auditing process but should be used only at the level of the business unit concerned.

There is also another issue that too few companies take into consideration, namely using only a limited number of "currency values" that can be applied in all four areas. Currently, performance is mainly measured in terms of dollars or euros; with the Balanced Scorecard this needs to be extended to include a (preferably consistent) measure of the quality of the company's relationships with its various stakeholders; and yet a third possible measure may be the 'time' dimension. An example of this type of Balanced Scorecard is shown in fig. 6.

Representation of a Company or Business Unit's Objective-setting System

- Early warning system instead of historical reporting
  - **Future-orientation**
- Identification of distinct objectives
  - **Balance**
- Concentration on key issues
  - **Focus**
- Converting company objectives into individual business unit objectives
  - **Universality**
- Quantification of objectives
  - **Measurability**

Fig. 5: Representation of an objective-setting system

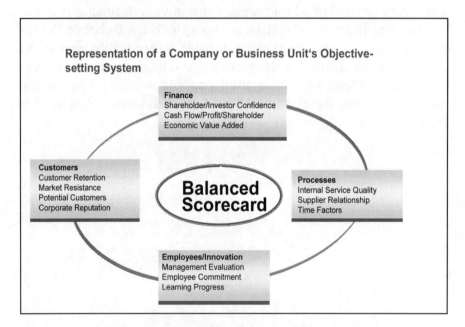

Fig. 6: Stakeholder Management underpins the Balanced Scorecard

13.1.5 Using the Balanced Scorecard

The Balanced Scorecard:

- is a tool that links a company's strategy and operational activity in a universal measurement system

- provides managers with a total picture based on financial and operational measurements

- contains a range of measurements that give an immediate and comprehensive overview of the company and its per-formance

- makes operational requirements and results transparently clear at a glance: that is, it shows how the company is performing in all areas simultaneously and facilitates goal-oriented management decision-making.

Fig. 7: The Balanced Scorecard

One of the biggest practical challenges in implementing a Balanced Scorecard approach is deciding whether it makes sense for different parts of a company to have their own individual Scorecards. Ultimately, the principle applies that each strategic business unit, with its sub-units, could have its own Balanced Scorecard: ideally, however, the optimal solution is to have a universal Balanced Scorecard that is applicable across the whole enterprise.

The Balanced Scorecard has particularly proved its worth in situations involving mergers/acquisitions or de-mergers/'carve-outs', by giving management a 360° view of the new organisation.

13.2 Construction of a Balanced Scorecard in the business environment

13.2.1 The essence of the Balanced Scorecard

The normal performance measurements – financial performance measured in terms of Dollars/Euros, and process efficiency measured in terms of time – can be left to one side for the moment. More important at this point is the measurement of the quality of stake-holder relationships.

Choice of indicators

Jack Welch, former CEO of General Electric and arguably the most successful manager of the last century, once said words to the effect that we have far too many measurements available to us in business and that in his opinion only three were sufficient to run any business in the world – cash flow, customer satisfaction and employee commitment.

This is no doubt the most basic version of a Balanced Scorecard in the world, but it nevertheless includes three of the four areas mentioned previously. What this also teaches us is that less is more: it is preferable to limit the number of indicators being worked with to 8-12 at the most.

In order to keep the explanation of relationship measurement as simple as possible, Jack Welch's shortened version of a Balanced Scorecard is used here, supplemented only by Internal Service Quality as a measure of business process quality, by Market Resistance as a measure of the potential for new customer acquisition and by Vitality as a measure of a company's ability to innovate.

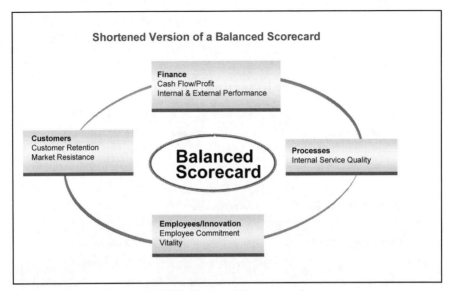

Fig. 8: Simple form of the Balanced Scorecard

13.2.2 The use of indices in the Balanced Scorecard

Customer Retention: Objectives
Customer retention has three objectives:

1. To strengthen relationships with existing customers, in order to retain them long-term.

2. To acquire new customers, and not just through recommendations by existing customers.

3. To increase the profitability of each and every individual customer relationship.

In order to achieve these three objectives, the internal audit function must have available to it a system that delivers business-relevant information, giving equal ('balanced') weight to the various measures it includes. For the first objective, it is necessary to have a measure of the customer relationship in the form of a single index that shows how the strength of this relationship varies - over time, for different customer groups, etc. (see Fig. 9). Only when customer loyalty is measured by a single index is it possible, in the context of a Balanced Scorecard, to give it the same priority as cash flow. It follows that Internal Service Quality (processes) and Employee Commitment also need to be measured in terms of similar indices.

Customer Retention		
ASPECTS	**QUESTIONS**	**RESULTS**
Rational	Overall Evaluation	Performance
Emotional	Recommendation	Satisfaction
Intentional	Repurchase	Retention Potential
Objective Barriers	Competitive Advantage	Retention Justification

Fig. 9: Customer Retention

Defining Customer Retention

For example, NFO Infratest measures Customer Retention using four questions, the answers to which are combined into a single index. On this index there are two 'limit values'. An index of 100 or more means that the company and its customers are in close partnership, virtually inseparable. From a competitive point of view, it is almost impossible to break into this relationship. An Index of 40 or below means that the relationship between the company and its customers is purely transactional and that customers are open to any offer from a competitor. Using such an index, which has been validated in more than 4,000 cases, gives the audit function the possibility of undertaking not only internal but also external benchmarking – that is, the company's performance can be bench-marked against other similar companies nation- or even world-wide. Any company can create its own index with different questions, as long as they are consistent over time so that performance improvements (or the opposite) are clearly identifiable, but such custom-designed indices are not of course capable of being bench-marked against other companies with different index constructions.

Employee Commitment / Internal Service Quality

The same applies to Employee Commitment (see fig. 10) and to Internal Service Quality (fig. 11). By using appropriate standardi-sed questions, indices can be calculated for other stakeholder groups in the Balanced Scorecard, with the same 40/100 'limit values' as for customers so that the performance of the company with regard to different stakeholder groups can be directly compared. The Euro-pean benchmarks, for example, show that Customer Loyalty (with an average index of 67) is distinctly higher than Employee Commit-ment (56) and Internal Service Quality (53).

Fig. 10: Employee Commitment questions

Internal Service Quality (ISQ)

ASPECTS	QUESTIONS	RESULTS
Emotional	Overall Evaluation	Satisfaction
Rational	Performance	Quality
Action-based	Usefulness	Support
Organizational	Need	Necessity

Fig. 11: Internal Service Quality questions

Such indices provide internal auditing with the means to broaden their perspective on both ongoing company management and forward planning beyond the usual financial criteria to include customers, process and employees.

However, concentrating on these numbers alone can lead to the second objective of Customer Retention – the acquisition of new customers - not being given the emphasis it requires.

13.2.3 Customer Typology and 'Market Resistance'

Customer Typology

In 1997, Jones and Sasser, both professors at the Harvard Business School, differentiated between four customer types – Apostles, Mercenaries, Hostages and Terrorists.

- Apostles are very satisfied and very loyal customers. They support the company by giving positive word-of-mouth recommendations to others. Experience shows that about 50% of a successful company's customers are Apostles.

- Dissatisfied and disloyal customers on the other hand – described by Jones and Sasser as Terrorists – are much more active than Apostles in giving negative recommendations against the company. In a given time period in which Apostles make 3 positive recommendations, Terrorists make 10 negative recommendations to either existing or potential customers.

- The percentage of customers that are Terrorists can be as high as 15%, even for successful companies.

- Customers described as Mercenaries are satisfied, but disloyal. They think that all products or services on offer are fundamentally the same and therefore tend to buy exclusively on price. They have no loyalty, they try to re-negotiate prices at every opportunity and are prepared to switch suppliers on the basis of just marginal price differences. About 25% of customers fall into this category.

- Customers who are dissatisfied but who see little possibility of changing suppliers due to a lack of alternatives, or due to contracts that tie them in, are described at Hostages.

Microsoft is a good example of this. A high percentage of Apostles who are enthusiastic about Microsoft is matched by a large group of Hostages who are dissatisfied but who see no cost-effective or practical alternative. For a long time this was also the case for purchasers of Gardena garden hoses. Because of the unique way that attachments are coupled together, once someone had bought one Gardena product they had to carry on buying other products from Gardena as well.

On average, about 10% of customers worldwide are Hostages (although this does of course vary between markets/suppliers that are monopolistic in some way and those that are highly competitive). If and when a Hostage comes across a supplier that can free them from this situation, they will in all likelihood switch suppliers even if the new one is no better than the existing one. The main motive is to escape from the constraint of being locked into a monopoly supplier and to have the opportunity to exercise choice.

This highly differentiating customer typology provides management with important information. Mercenaries require a different strategy from Apostles; Hostages require a different strategy from Terrorists.

Whilst this information supports management decision-taking, it is too complex to use for strategic audit control purposes. The fact that Terrorists make 10 negative recommendations in the same time that Apostles make 3 positive ones means that a 'Market Resistance' indicator can be calculated that shows the potential for new customer acquisition (see fig. 12). Given that, on average, a successful company is likely to have something more than three times as many Apostles as Terrorists, the equilibrium value of this indicator is 1.0, at which point a normal level of marketing activity is sufficient. If the Market Resistance indicator is greater than 1.0, the negative word-of-mouth from the Terrorists is outweighing the positive word-of-mouth from the Apostles, and the company must invest more in its marketing/sales activities in order to acquire sufficient numbers of new customers to counteract this situation; if, on the other hand, the value of the indicator is less than 1.0, the Apostles are outweighing the Terrorists and the company can choose whether to leave things as they are or whether to reduce its investment in marketing/sales.

There are comparable typologies for the Employee Commitment and Internal Customer Satisfaction measures, which are of great interest to the H.R. function but again too detailed for strategic management.

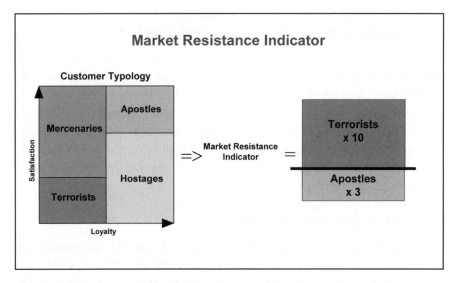

Fig. 12: Market resistance

13.2.4 "Vitality" – making things happen

Quality elements

These approaches still do not solve the problem of how to increase profitability through Customer Retention.

At the end of the 1980s Harvard University conducted an extensive study on how many aspects of a product (or 'quality elements') consumers can evaluate, and established that even a simple product such as an ice-lolly has 64 different quality elements. One only has to think of such areas as taste, ingredients, quality of the chocolate, attractiveness of the packaging, ease of opening the packaging, consistency, freshness and reliability of the refrigerated distribution chain, image, price and so on. An ice-cream manufacturer that wants to be better than the competition on all 64 aspects only has two choices:

- If he performs better on all aspects and maintains price-competitiveness against the competition, he will soon be deprived of any hope of being profitable.

- If he sells his premium product at a sufficiently high price for it to be profitable, it will attract only a small minority of the potential market and become a niche product.

In reality, experience shows that the consumer only takes a few aspects into account when making a purchase decision. For the ice-cream manufacturer it is therefore essential to know which out of all the theoretical quality elements are the most relevant to the consumer. And since most products are more complex than an ice-lolly, and no doubt have more criteria by which they might potentially be evaluated, establishing which criteria are the really relevant ones becomes all-important.

Importance of quality elements

When analysing the relative importance of quality elements, the question arises as to how to measure 'importance'. When people are asked directly what they think is important, they tend to give answers that are rational and/or conditioned by social acceptability, which are different from the results obtained by indirect analysis of their behavioural motives. For example, if airline passengers are asked how important they think 'pilot competence' is, they will inevitably say it is extremely important; however, analysis of their actual behaviour shows that passengers rarely base their choice of airline on pilot competence, because all major airlines are thought to have pilots with the same (high) level of competence.

It a matrix is constructed using these two definitions of the importance of the quality elements – verbally stated importance and their actual impact on behaviour – it becomes clear that there are four different types of quality elements (see fig. 13).

- Motivators – important to communicate (to respond to customers' belief in their importance) and do impact on behaviour.

- Hygienics – important to communicate but do not impact on behaviour.

- Hidden Opportunities – not thought to be as important as other quality elements but do impact on behaviour.

- Potentials?/Savers? – neither thought to be as important as other quality elements nor impact on behaviour.

Hidden Opportunities

Hidden Opportunities can best be illustrated by the case of the airline SAS. At the beginning of the 1980s, SAS was in considerable difficulties when Jan Carlsson took over as Chief Executive. His first decision was to cancel all orders for new aircraft, and to offer passengers smoked salmon and champagne instead. When market researchers asked passengers how important free champagne was to them, the answer came back as "not important at all". However, the same passengers started to use SAS more frequently because they saw free champagne as a desirable luxury and as a point of differentiation between SAS and its competitors.

In a market economy, companies continuously try to find 'hidden opportunities'. They think about which products and services, or rather which aspects of them, they can exploit to improve their retention of existing customers and to attract new customers. An innovative company distinguishes itself from its competitors by continuously seeking out and building on these hidden opportunities.

As this strategy proved to be successful, Jan Carlsson sought out other new quality elements around the 'free champagne' idea – such as the quality of the in-flight meals, seat width, distance between seats, and so on – and developed and marketed it as the 'Business Class' package. As other airlines followed suit and passengers began to recognise its value, its perceived (stated) importance increased and it became a Motivator rather than a Hidden Opportunity.

As a rule, successful companies know what motivates their customers. It is important that customers' expectations are fully met – and Motivators that are clearly better fulfilled by a company than by its competitors become that company's USPs (Unique Selling Propositions). An inadequately fulfilled Motivator runs a high risk of causing customers to defect: however, improving performance on items in the Motivator area is also generally high-cost since the competition will also be investing in improving their performance on the same issues.

154

Returning to the Business Class case, airlines came to realise that, although passengers still thought it to be important, few of them actually chose which airline to use on this basis since they were all broadly similar, so Business Class became a Hygienic. And on domestic flights at least, free champagne and elaborate meals could be eliminated as a cost saving measure without impacting on passenger volumes. In the future, perhaps, free champagne might disappear from people's horizons altogether and this quality element will therefore become totally irrelevant (an actual 'Saver') – although the concept in some other form might well then come back again at a later date as a 'new' Hidden Opportunity.

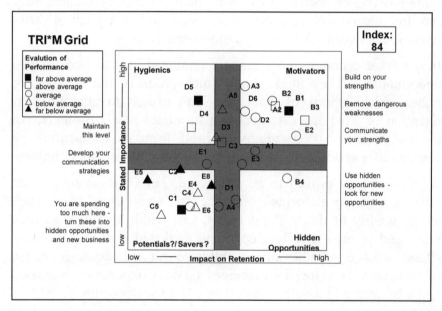

Fig. 13: TRI*M Grid

The life-cycle of quality elements

This example illustrates the life-cycle of quality elements. New quality elements that companies develop start off as Hidden Opportunities (or even as question marks in the bottom-left Potentials?/Savers? quadrant of the matrix – particularly future product issues, the relevance of which is not yet apparent in the market place); they then become Motivators and then Hygienics; and then at some point lose their significance altogether. One must, however, be aware that there are usually some things that one might describe as 'structural' aspects of a particular market – things that are absolutely indispensable but which all competitors do well and which therefore do not differentiate between competitors. In the case of the major airlines, 'pilot competence' would be one such issue.

An opposite development can occur with quality elements that derive from societal pressures, such as environmental issues. These were initially Hygienics (everybody talked about them, but nobody wanted to pay for them), but now they are often Motivators.

The same sort of analysis can be applied to the quality elements that determine Employee Commitment and Internal Service Quality. These analyses are extremely useful, both for management and for the internal audit function, since they provide an essential basis on which to take action on internal staff/organisational/process issues. However, the differences in the quality elements that apply in different functions/departments of a company make them non-comparable across functions/departments and inappropriate for strategic performance measurement.

Based on these analysis procedures (Grid analysis of Customer Retention, Employee Commitment and Internal Service Quality) NFO has developed a 'Vitality Index' which shows the auditor how dynamic the company is, at a departmental or business unit level, in terms of the rate of conversion of Hidden Opportunities into Motivators and the rate of performance improvement on Motivator quality elements. This Vitality Index is extremely valuable in the context of strategic management because it shows to what extent a department or business unit is actively working towards improving its position, or whether it is just adopting a passive stance towards the challenges that face it.

13.2.5 The Balanced Scorecard for business units without direct customer contact

The performance of departments that do not have direct customer contact can also be measured in terms of the four areas that apply to customer-facing departments. For such departments, the Balanced Scorecard can show not only their Internal Service Quality ratings but also the evaluations of external clients (see fig. 14).

The way this is done is to bundle together the quality elements for which a particular department is responsible and to attribute a 'Customer Retention Index' to this department based on the company's performance on these particular quality elements compared with its performance on all quality elements. This gives an Index which is department-specific and directly comparable with the overall company Index. In this way, indices can also be developed for departments that have no, or only indirect, customer contact.

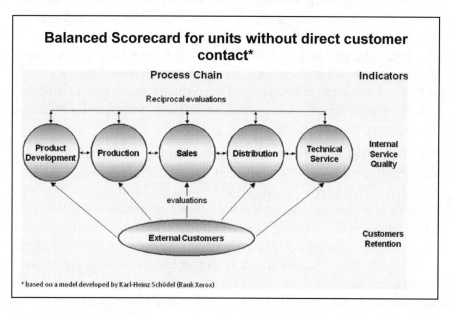

Fig. 14: Process chain

This extension to the implementation of the Balanced Scorecard will be elaborated upon in more detail in a future article.

13.3 Conclusion

The Balanced Scorecard constitutes an excellent platform for broadening performance measurement within a company for facilitating both internal and external benchmarking, and for optimising strategic management, operational management and the internal audit function.

14 Increasing Customer Loyalty in Markets Faced with Changing Customer Expectations

Shubhra Ramchandani

14.1 Introduction

The last couple of years have been particularly difficult for the ubiquitous American *fast food* restaurant. The sluggish economy and concerns for employment have certainly exacerbated the problems of this sector already plagued by change. The success of the "franchise" model over the last couple of decades was based on the offer to the customer of a limited number of pre-defined menu choices available at a guaranteed level of consistency, quality and price. Today, the call is for personalization, "rightsizing" and eating healthily, as eating out is becoming more of a routine necessity for the majority of Americans versus the special occasion it used to be. The familiar fast food restaurants are seeing increasing competition not just from other similar restaurants, but also from the increasing number of "take home", "restaurant quality" prepared meal options. Manufacturers of eat-at-home food options are striving to capture the fine dining experience of the restaurant. Restaurants are striving to capture the comfort, convenience, choices and conviviality of family and friends sitting around the kitchen table eating their favourite food, prepared just the way they like it, served lovingly and attentively by the ultimate cook and waitperson, just like Mom! So, while the consumer is demanding (and getting) an abundance of choices and options, restaurants cannot count on the free spending, naturally expanding eating-out customer pools of the 90's; they must now focus on retaining and growing market-share through increasing spend-per-meal and repeat business, in other words, on improving customer loyalty.

14.2   NFO Research

NFO designed and conducted a research study to identify the impact of changing consumer expectations on customer loyalty to the top ten restaurant chains within three different restaurant categories: *Quick Serve, Fast Casual and Full Serve*. The study was conducted in the summer of 2003 from a nationally representative sample of consumers. Over 600 consumers were asked to rate the performance of restaurants they visited most often in the last two months. These restaurants were grouped into three categories: *Quick Service, Fast Casual* and *Full Service* restaurants based on classifications published by the restaurant industry. The survey was conducted among members of NFO's Interactive panel of more than one million U.S. households.

14.3 Research findings

Overall the restaurant sector is exceeding customer expectations

Overall, the increased competition within the sector has created a real "win" for consumer. The restaurant industry receives an A- or a TRI*M Index of 85 out of an achievable score of 100, from consumers who are eating out on a regular basis. This grade was based on a TRI*M Index developed from consumer responses to four questions.

1. How would you rate the overall performance of (restaurant visited most often), based on your experience with their food and services?

2. How likely are you to recommend their food and services to others?

3. How likely are you to visit (this restaurant) in the future?

4. How would you rate the advantage of having a meal at (this restaurant) compared to having a meal at a similar restaurant?

With a TRI*M Index of 85, the restaurant sector falls in the top third of service providers in North America, according to the 2003

TRI*M Database of approximately 750,000 customer interviews conducted over the most recent three year period in North America.

Our findings also show that the restaurant industry commands an impressive degree of advocacy – over 60% of restaurant goers are true advocates of their favourite restaurants (highly satisfied and loyal), with only 23 % critics (highly dissatisfied). About half of those dissatisfied continue to frequent the restaurant based on a lack of alternatives.

Top drivers of consumer preference for the restaurants they frequent most often

To identify the primary drivers of consumer preference for a particular restaurant they patronize we asked them to rate their preferred restaurant on the following aspects and also to state how important each aspect was to them:

Restaurant atmosphere is enjoyable
Restaurant is in touch with the special needs of customers
Restaurant is conveniently located
Menu includes meals that suit my tastes and preferences
Menu offers an adequate variety of choices
Menu items are available as described
Temperature of my food
Menu offers enough options for well-balanced, nutritious meal choices
Service staff is knowledgeable and able to answer questions
Waiting times (e.g. being seated, drive-thru line, placing an order, being served food) are reasonable
Service staff is friendly and polite
Service staff shows pride in the restaurant

Prices are comparable to similar restaurants
Restaurant provides a good value for the money
Offers promotions, specials or rewards programs that I am interested in

Note: We asked restaurant goers to rate their favorite restaurant on the above 15 dimensions on a scale of Excellent, Very Good, Good, Fair and Poor; as well as telling us how important each attribute was to them when they select a restaurant to eat. On a scale of: Extremely important to not at all important.

Results of the responses to the above questions can be viewed as both good news and bad news. While food (quality, variety), reasonable prices and convenient location are top drivers of consumer preference for specific restaurants they choose to frequent, almost all major restaurant operators are performing at above average levels in these three dimensions. This essentially means that the consumer can be selective and receive the quality of food desired at a reasonable price at a location that is accessible, from many different restaurants.

So, why are restaurant operators feeling the pressure to improve in order to retain customer loyalty?

Mostly because some of their own are setting higher standards in hopes of winning customers away. Consider, for example, the emerging *Fast Casual* category that outperforms both the *Quick Service* and the *Full Service* categories with a high A+ rating (TRI*M Index of 105). *Quick Service* restaurants as a whole only receive a B rating (TRI*M Index of 81). Within *Quick Service*, the variability is significant as well – with the low performers getting a C- to D rating (TRI*M Index of around 66). On average, *Fast Casual* category restaurants have less than 5% dissatisfied customers. Compare this to the 27% dissatisfied customers for the *Quick Service* category as a whole and 37% dissatisfied customers for poor performing restaurants within *Quick Service*. For the under performing restaurants the message is clear - either shape up or face the consequences of market share erosion - because not only will dissatisfied customers vote with their feet, they will also tell at least 10 people they know about how they feel!

As can be seen in fig. 1 below, performance by top drivers of preference varies by restaurant category

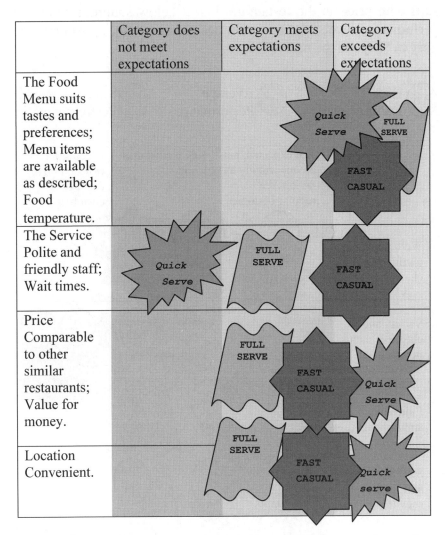

Fig. 1: How each restaurant segment is meeting expectations of their regular customers in top drivers of customer preference...?

164

Study results also provided consumer feedback on features that are being considered by many of the top restaurant chains as possible opportunities to strengthen customer loyalty and grow market share, including: well-balanced nutritious meal choices, variety and choice of menu items, enjoyable restaurant atmosphere and knowledgeable staff with pride in the restaurant. Fig. 2 below summarizes current performance levels and opportunities presented, by restaurant category in "beyond the basics" items:

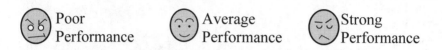

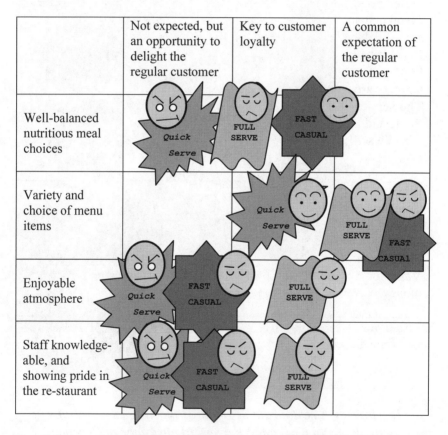

Fig. 2: Beyond the basics…What do customers think of the menu and service enhancements being offered…?

From the results above, it is apparent that the strategic priorities for restaurants have been menu selection, price promotions and expanding the number of outlets. These factors continue to be key to retaining customer loyalty, however, with generally strong performance by most restaurants in these areas, they do not support a strategy of differentiation in a highly competitive market. Service dimensions, including restaurant atmosphere, provide an opportunity for the industry as a whole to keep their regular customers coming back. Consumers want a sense of personal attention, engagement, ownership and pride in the restaurants they regularly visit. On the surface this seems pretty basic. Our study results, however, show that many restaurants have lost touch with this core value proposition of high quality service because of their drive to be "different" as well as "all things to all people" has obscured the prime directive of ensuring a pleasant experience for all restaurant customers.

How can restaurants create increased customer loyalty through repeat business?

In the highly competitive and commoditized American market in which the top restaurant chains compete, merely to survive restaurants have to perform well on the basic drivers of consumer preference – food, price and location. Promotions, specials and rewards may help create short-term spikes but do not motivate regular customers to return. The prescription for success lies in first ensuring that basic customer expectations are being met at acceptable levels, and then moving on to create differentiation through taking advantage of hidden opportunities of delighting the customer. Of course, the recipe for success will vary by restaurant. However, some category level recommendations are noted in table 1 below:

Table 1

A prescription for increasing customer loyalty – by category…

Quick Serve	Fast Casual	Full Serve
First: Improve basic service skills of staff; Reduce wait times. *Second*, Improve restaurant atmosphere and experience.	*First,* Add locations, without impacting current service levels; improve menu variety and choice. *Second*: create an enjoyable restaurant atmosphere and experience	Focus on excelling in service to justify price levels.

Attachment – Restaurant Categories

Following is a list of the of restaurants categorized into each of the 3 categories

Quick Serve	Fast Casual	Full Service
McDonald's	Boston Market	Applebee's
Burger King	Panera Bread	Red Lobster
Wendy's	St. Louis Bread	Outback Steakhouse
Taco Bell	Fazoli's	Chili's Bar & Grill
Subway	Fuddrucker's	Olive Garden
Arby's	Au Bon Pain	TGI Fridays
Dairy Queen	Souplantation	Ruby Tuesday
Jack in the Box	Sweet Tomatoes	Bennegan's
Hardee's		Macaroni Grill
Sonic Drive-In		Hooters

Authors

Andreas Capell has been working with Haspa (Hamburger Sparkasse) since April 1993. He is responsible for the development of the quality management processes as well as the realization on all levels of Haspa. He is also responsible for the market research at Haspa.

Chapter 2

Brian Digby is Executive Vice President, Marketing. He leads a team of marketing professionals in developing product and distribution strategies for ATB, as well as managing the corporate brand. Marketing initiatives and activities include product management, advertising and promotions, community relations, sponsorships, and market research. Brian also leads ATB's strategic and business planning. Brian is a Director of MasterCard Canada Inc.

Chapter 8

Elke Himmelsbach, Director NFO Infratest International Financial Research has 12 years experience in financial research with focus on Stakeholder Management and Brand Management. She is responsible for the establishment of international financial research business and the set-up and coordination of global research projects. She has published several articles and given speeches on financial topics.

Chapter 3

Dr. Margit Huber, Business Area Manager at NFO Infratest Wirtschaftsforschung is responsible for international market research surveys especially in the area of Customer Satisfaction in the B2B Industry and Employee Commitment. In addition she is in charge for the group's network of more than 250 consultants working in the area of Stakeholder Management.

Chapter 13

Graham Hurst is responsible for Market Research at Orange in Switzerland since 1999. Graham Hurst started his professional carreer in Switzerland. After running his own market research agency, he moved client side and worked as Market Research manager for well known international companies such as Reynolds Tobacco, Givaudan, and Energizer.

Chapter 6

Ian Jarvis is a Senior Consultant at NFO WorldGroup, UK. In addition, he is responsible for Knowledge Management within the Stakeholder Management area.

Chapter 13

Andre Kremser, B.Sc. Administrative Science, was from 1994 to 1996 Staff Manager at Südwestdeutsche Landesbank. Since 1996 at BW-Bank in Personnel Department he is responsible for Change Management and Human Resources projects.

Chapter 10

Sanjeev Luther is Administrative Vice President of M&T Bank. He is charged with creating initiatives, programs and processes to drive Customer-Centric philosophy, including enhancing the quality of customer information and fostering corporate utilization of customer and competitive information to guide planning and decision-making. Led creation of Center of Excellence for Retail Information Services/ Consumer and Competitive Insights, developed and led implementation of measurement evaluation programs for Consumer Marketing and promotional programs that provide strategic insights for retail business areas throughout the bank.

Chapter 12

Dr. Martin Platzer joined voestalpine Schienen GmbH at the end of 1999 as Senior Vice President Sales, and was appointed to his present position in 2001 after the establishment of voestalpine Bahnsysteme as the holding company for the voestalpine railway system group.

Chapter 4

Shubhra Ramchandani is the North American Practice Leader for Stakeholder Relationship Management. Shubhra's experience spans several industries including financial services, information services and manufacturing. More recently she has worked with a variety of multi-national consumer goods manufacturers.

Chapter 14

Horst Schäfers is Managing Executive of ISIS Multimedia Net GmbH, Düsseldorf. In 1994 he founded ISIS Multimedia Net, the first German city-wide and regional carrier. Besides that he is Vice President of BREKO, Federal Association of Regional and Local Telecommunications Operators and a member of the Industrial Committee of the Chamber of Industry and Commerce.

Chapter 9

Dr. Joachim Scharioth is Managing Director of NFO Infratest Wirtschaftsforschung, a subsidiary of NFO WorldGroup. He is responsible for the Group's offering in the Stakeholder Management area worldwide.

Chapter 13

Lenka Šilerová worked after her graduation as a research executive in multimedia research. Since 1997 has been with Eurotel Prague, first as a market research specialist, at present leading a market research and analysis team. In 2003 successfully finished a Ph.D. program in social psychology.

Chapter 5

Christine Theodorovics is head of the quality management of the Credit Suisse in Zurich. Her main task is the improvement of service quality through optimal complaint management and customer retention analyses as well as process improvements. Before that she worked for the NFO WordGroup for 5 years in the Stakeholder Management area. Since 1997 she is a speaker in the business excellence area.

Chapter 7

Dr. Wolfgang Werner works for the 'Corporate Human Resources and Social Policies' Department of Degussa AG in Düsseldorf, Germany and is responsible for major HR Projects and international personnel work. He worked for several chemical corporations gaining experience in different functions including Quality Management, Organizational Development and Internal Management Consulting. He is active in the steering committees of German institutions like DGQ, DIN, VCI, TÜVCert.

Chapter 11

Robert A. Wieland, Director of NFO Infra-test, is in charge for the market segment "banks & building societies". He is responsible for the price & product managemet system NFO VALUE●MANAGER. He has had seve-ral publications and public speaches on finan-cial topics.

Chapter 3

Pauline Williams began her career in Market Research with NOP some 17 years ago. Her first clientside role was heading up DHL UK, followed by British Gas and now Nationwide. She set up the first Best Clientside Practice project with Steve Wills 3 years ago. This provided the industry with a handbook which enabled new Market Research functions to be set up effectively and for existing ones to take a check on their efficiency. The second Best Clientside Practice project has been set up by Pauline and Steve to move this work on – to assist Market Research functions to add real value to their businesses.

Chapter 1

Druck: Strauss Offsetdruck, Mörlenbach
Verarbeitung: Schäffer, Grünstadt